The Bottom Lines 2016

52 Unforgettable Lessons in Leadership

Tom Zender

ISBN: 1516980239
ISBN 13: 9781516980239
Library of Congress Control Number: 2015918092
CreateSpace Independent Publishing Platform
North Charleston, South Carolina

Endorsements for *The Bottom Lines 2016*

Tom's book has numerous bite-size pieces of wisdom for quick and easy consumption from which I learned a lot. Tom offers many real world examples that help the brain paint a detailed picture for more effective learning. Reading the entire book can be great orientation to becoming a leader. Reading one or more lessons a night can end the day on a positive note and prime the sleeping brain for positive learning. I enjoy humor (Lesson 9) to relax and encourage creativity. I totally agree with Tom's law to start humor by laughing at myself, not others.

Barbara Luther, a member of the national firm NewLAWu.s., has been helping creative people for more than a quarter of a century protect and profit from their names and ideas. A skilled patent attorney, she also obtains trademark and copyright protection for her clients. She enjoys hearing new ideas and putting clients at ease with a little self-deprecating humor.

■ ■ ■

What a perfect title for this book! As a family that has owned numerous businesses, I guarantee that anyone who follows Tom's teachings will improve their bottom line. The most important lesson learned is centuries old, "Bleeders are arrogant and think they know everything. Leaders are humble and credit their people and others." Wisdom to know the difference opens the trail to success.

Ernest Garfield is President of Independent Bank Developers, LLC and Chairman of Interstate Bank Developers, Inc. He is also the founder of the Alliance of Business Banks and the Community Bank Advisory Council for Arizona members of Congress. The Phoenix Business Journal recognized him as one of the most influential Arizona business leaders of 2007.

■   ■   ■

For many years I have collected *"How To"* business books. I have finally found the best! If you read Tom Zender's *The Bottom Lines: 2016*, you will find easy to read pages that will guide you to entrepreneurial success. You will learn how to confront and overcome anxiety and fear which are major Impediments you will encounter as you pursue success. Lesson 29 deals with "Trust". This is the most important part of any and all relationships in your personal and business life. So trust me, you will love this book!

Donald C. Hannah is an experienced serial entrepreneur dealing in maritime and real estate ventures in the USA and overseas. He was a finalist for an Inc. Magazine Entrepreneur of the Year award.

Dedication

The Bottom Lines: 2016 is dedicated to all of the remarkable CEO's and business mentors who have enriched my career by sharing their wisdom, providing their unselfish guidance, and by giving their steadfast devotion to my success. I deeply thank you, always.

This book also is dedicated to Eliances, where successful business leaders and mentors align with entrepreneurs to help them build better businesses. My gratitude overflows for David Cogan, the founder and facilitator, and to all the members of Eliances.

Likewise, I am indebted to my wife, Dr. Wendy Zender, Ph.D., and so many business friends who have supported me in creating *The Bottom Lines.*

Table of Contents

Foreword

I f you ever have the good fortune to meet with Tom Zender you will notice a few things right away.

You know going in that he's an accomplished business leader and mentor with an impressive record of success and achievements. His resume speaks for itself.

But what you also discover is this: He's sincere and authentic. He is humble, kind and appreciates being in your company. He's a good listener. If he has an ego, he hides it well.

He's a role model leader.

And now that you have the good fortune to get your hands on this book, I think you will notice a few things right way.

That's right, all of Tom's characteristics come though loud and clear in his writing as well.

That's a rare fete and not one that I've observed much in many years of mingling and mentoring with the top business leaders in our community.

I've seen leaders with Tom's traits who can't quite carry off the message when it comes to their writing. They don't have the ability to write from their hearts as much as from their heads.

And I've seen leaders without Tom's traits who can't carry off the message because they don't live the values they write about, and you can't fool all of the people all of the time.

Tom's book of 52 lessons provides a wonderful source of inspiration and knowledge across a wide range of topics that are relevant to leaders in just about any walk of life these days.

I know you will find this to be a source of inspiration, motivation and determination as you grow as a leader. I hope you enjoy the book, as well as your leadership journey.

Don Henninger, principal of DH Advisors, had a 37-year career in the newspaper business, serving as CEO/Publisher of the Phoenix Business Journal for 15 years, as well as Managing Editor of The Arizona Republic and other newsroom jobs before that.

Preface

I am a Professional CEO Mentor. I meet amazing leaders and others along the way, and learn valuable lessons in the process. And, throughout my business career, I have collected hundreds of business lessons from my mentors, managers, and others. These teachings are brief and simple. And powerful.

This book is intended to share some of the best lessons I have learned with a wide audience of business people – leaders, managers, and others. You.

Instead of the typically laborious, business writings that we see, I decided that a more conversational way of business wisdom is easier and more interesting to read and remember. Brevity counts. So does a touch of humor. You'll see.

My business path began with General Electric and Honeywell, crossed through midsize and startup companies, took a spin in a nonprofit organization, and landed as a professional CEO mentor and author. My leadership roles included CEO, senior VP, manager, supervisor, and individual contributor. I held responsibility for every business function, including marketing, sales, technology development, financial, HR, production, and facilities. I also served on the boards of NASDAQ and Toronto Stock Exchange companies – and on several nonprofit boards. I had a taste of everything on the broad buffet of business. Mostly satisfying. With some heartburn, too.

The Bottom Lines: 2016 includes hard, easy, unexpected, fun, and other kinds of lessons. Above all, they are practical for building better business. Proven stuff.

Now, you can read and benefit from such penetrating insights as:

- Leaders and bleeders: the art of building and killing businesses
- Infinite shades of gray: the new management mind
- The company bus: on it, under it, or off it
- Why high flying businesses stall in midair
- Simplifiers and complicators: leadership uncluttered
- How to avoid death by meaningless meetings
- Seven easy steps to more creativity in the workplace

Each lesson ends with a short summary. Here is the one for *Simplifiers and complicators: leadership uncluttered:*

THE BOTTOM LINES

Un-complicate. Design and develop simplicity into products, services, and processes. Teach teams to go for the uncluttered. Don't introduce complexity. View things from the perspective of a user. Make it simple. Keep it simple.

Acknowledgements

Thank you, all of my durable business mentors, including: Bob Geronime, Ken Fisher, Dr. Kirk Thompson, Bob Connors, Curt Hare, Bill Patton, Webb Castor, Rowland Thomas, Bruce Schall, Fred Anderson, and many others who led, suggested, and sometimes cajoled me along my path of success in business. And, who taught me to mentor others. My giveback.

Also, thanks to those "anti-mentors" who unwittingly convinced me about those behaviors that I do not want to copy. Ever.

I acknowledge a long list of business education professors, instructors, and facilitators who not only taught me the bricks of business, but also filled in the spaces with the mortar of real experience – most especially Dr. Fred Zook and Cal Milan.

There have been many adept authors of business books and publications that strongly influenced me: Peter Drucker, Steven Covey, Joseph Jaworski, Ken Blanchard, Dale Carnegie, Jim Collins, Marcus Buckingham, Og Mandingo, Napoleon Hill, and endless others.

I thank many business and personal friends for giving me sustained encouragement to bring *The Bottom Lines* to business (and other) readers who constantly seek creative ways to improve their leadership, businesses, careers, jobs, and work.

Thank you to the team at CreateSpace, Kindle Direct Publishing, and Amazon for your focused and expert assistance in helping me to transform this book from a vision into a reality.

Oh, yes. My wife, chief supporter, and editor, Dr. Wendy Zender, Ph.D., University of Southern California. Wendy is gifted in helping me craft words, sentences, paragraphs, and punctuation into something readable. She should be. She is a graduate university professor who reads a continuous stream of doctoral level theses from her students. I think I am one of them!

About the Author

Tom Zender is a Professional CEO Mentor in Phoenix, Arizona.

He held leadership roles at General Electric and Honeywell, and has been a senior vice president in publicly held corporations, New York Stock Exchange and NASDAQ listed. Tom was the CEO of a startup technology company and he was president and CEO of a global nonprofit which serves over two million people globally.

His corporate board experience includes NASDAQ, Toronto Stock Exchange, and OTC listed public companies. Tom held nonprofit board positions with Ottawa University and the Forum for Corporate Directors.

In his CEO and senior vice president roles he held profit and loss responsibility for every business function.

Tom writes weekly for a professional business publication on a voluntary basis, mentors students at Arizona State University's

SkySong startup business incubator, and is an advisor to Paradise Valley Community College.

He has spoken to business audiences of over 1,000 people in more than 30 countries.

Tom Zender is a graduate of Ottawa University with a B.A. in Business with focus areas of Leadership, Marketing, and Information Technology.

His prior two published books were Amazon bestseller e-books about business ethics:

- *God Goes to Work* was among the top ten e-books in business ethics listed by Amazon.com. Published in 2010 by John Wiley & Sons, it was widely distributed in the United States, Canada, the UK, Australia, and India.
- *One-Minute Meditations at Work*, Published by Hay House/Balboa Press, it was among the top 5% of all e-books sold by Amazon.com.

Tom Zender
tomzender@me.com
www.tomzendermentor.com

Lesson: 1

Leaders and bleeders: the art of building and killing businesses

In leadership, every leader wants to be a good one. But, many are not. Bad leaders practice "bleedership" and can ruin otherwise promising businesses. There are numerous, well publicized characteristics of strong leaders. What about the earmarks of bad leaders ("bleeders")? Read on.

Leaders are builders. They build up people and organizations, and support all their stakeholders: employees, customers, vendors, their management teams, and their communities. And, they foster creative innovation for great products and services. They are winners.

Bleeders are wreckers. They tear down people and organizations, and manipulate stakeholders. Their primary bottom line is only about profits, and their people are expendable. The bleeder's initial products and services may be attractive, but often fall behind in subsequent renditions. They are losers.

BLEEDERS AND LEADERS

Contrasting bleeders with leaders gives great insight into how to be a good leader - and avoid being a bad bleeder. And, if you think you might have some weak leadership qualities, this contrast can help you do some self-mending.

Bleeders are micro-managers because they do not trust others.
Leaders are macro-managers because they effectively delegate with trust.

Bleeders do not have empathy for others.
Leaders respect how their employees and others think and feel.

Bleeders serve themselves.
Leaders serve others.

Bleeders order others around without respect.
Leaders build good followers and empower them.

Bleeders are inept at judging character, including their own.
Leaders see good character in others and engage them for success.

Bleeders fear change.
Leaders welcome positive change and foster it.

Bleeders are arrogant and believe that they know everything.
Leaders are humble and give credit to their people and others.

Bleeders lack vision and demand that others blindly follow.
Leaders have a clear vision and attract others to be part of it.

Bleeders have an unbalanced life, burn out, and create chaos.
Leaders have good work-life balance and promote it for others

Bleeders perform poorly or not at all.
Leaders establish success through proven performance, not promise.

THERE IS MORE ...

Bleeders are poor communicators and others are left in the dark.
Leaders communicate clearly (spoken, written, listening) with everyone.

Bleeders either set muddy expectations, or have no expectations.
Leaders establish goals and objectives, and communicate them.

Bleeders promote themselves.
Leaders promote others.

Bleeders blow with the wind and give in too easily from weakness.
Leaders stand for their principles and successfully negotiate from strength.

Bleeders are disorganized.
Leaders organize people, programs, and projects.

Bleeders over promise and under deliver.
Leaders under promise and over deliver.

Bleeders order others around without respect.
Leaders build good followers and empower them.

Bleeders have fear.
Leaders have faith.

Clearly, the positive qualities of a good leader offer an increased opportunity to build sustainable success for their organizations - far more than a bad bleeder and their poor to non-existent success, both short and long term.

THE BOTTOM LINES

Stop bleeding. Give up any negative qualities of bleeders. Adopt all the characteristics of good leaders. These abilities can be learned, practiced, and developed. Build great organizations and sustain them. Start leading.

Lesson: 2

Infinite shades of gray: the new management mind

Black or white thinking has been the way of western business culture for centuries. On or off, in or out, good or bad has been our conventional, polarized way of looking at business issues and opportunities. Call it dualistic thinking. It served us well for centuries in our highly ordered business world. But, it is in decay because there is a better way.

Non-dual, or integral, thinkers see both – black and white, on and off, good and bad. They see infinite shades of gray between black and white – instead of a rigid black or white perspective.

Leaders, managers, and individuals who transform to the more relaxed and effective mode of the non-dual thinking path see, know and practice effective traits in the emerging new world of business.

WHAT KILLED KODAK?

A pileup of great American corporations decayed in the dump of hierarchical, one-way polarized thinking - dualistic thinking. The road to their long-ago success is now littered with the rusted-out company busses and their locked steering wheels against change. Employees were thrown under the bus and leaders parachuted out of the bus. That ride is over.

WHAT GESTATED GOOGLE?

Flexible turns on the speedway to success birthed the new corporation. And the pivot point is based upon more leaders, managers, and employees adopting non-dual, integral thinking. This new company bus is on a roll, with new leader-drivers and every seat occupied by happy employee-riders. This ride is thrilling.

THE WORLD OF
NON-DUAL LEADERS

Rather than the polarized "either/or" of the dualistic view, the non-dual thinker sees the business world from a "both/and" perspective:

- They see options and alternatives.
- They progress by influencing events and inspiring people.
- They know that every one-sided solution is predestined to fail.
- They learn to work together with others for solutions.
- They know that dilemmas happen because of fearful, fixed positions.
- They search for middle ground, win-win solutions.
- They know that there are no perfect solutions, only optimum solutions.
- They avoid polarity and all-or-none thinking.

- They know that rapid recourse to hard rules is often just a sign of laziness.
- They see that adhering to rigid rules can avoid real responsibility.
- They believe that wisdom is "the art of the possible."
- They keep offering new data, until getting some consensus from all sides.
- They have an ability to care beyond their own personal advantage.
- They do not seek to quickly get a problem off the plate – they seek to achieve good for the largest number, now and into the future.
- They want to increase both freedom and ownership among the group, not just subservience, which will ultimately sabotage the work anyway.
- They let people know the "why" of a decision, and show how that is consistent with the group's values.

Some of these ideas are adapted from the 2009 book by Richard Rohr, *The Naked Now*. Crossroad Publishing Company: NY.

Integral thinking leaders know that compromise and consensus does not abdicate values, but can find other values such as community building and giving more people a personal investment in outcomes.

THE BOTTOM LINES
Abandon black OR white thinking. Adopt black AND white, gray thinking. Be an integral, non-dual business leader. Seek options and be flexible. Build consensus teams that get into the company bus and burn rubber. Go gray, go fast.

Lesson: 3

The whole leader: mind, body, soul, and guts

So you are a leader and you think that you need some balance - of something or some things. You might think that it is a balance of experience, management, prior successes, and a full slate of all things business. The "outer us." OK, but the other part of your abilities-equation has to do with a higher level of personal qualities. What are they?

Mind, Body and Soul quadrants are often used to describe the "inner us," and there is an overdose of books, seminars, and organizations that teach and promote that idea. "Guts" gets added as a quadrant, not as an expression of courage, but as descriptive of our feelings. These four quadrants when balanced and integrated are our inner force – and most powerful when blended with our business strengths.

If any of the quadrants is weak, the whole leader is diminished. Power-less. Fortunately, there are symptoms and solutions for rebalancing our "inner us" quadrants: Mind, Body, Soul, Guts.

MIND
Symptoms - when we are off track mentally/intellectually, our knowledge can be unclear, fuzzy or seem missing. We can struggle to match solutions to problems, and not even be able to dissect and define a problem. Perhaps we feel out of date with our information.

Solutions - take a course or go to a seminar for updates, read material that refreshes our knowledge base, be a life-long-learner, do some research, talk to others who have information we need, take on more challenging tasks.

BODY
Symptoms - we experience a stream of minor illnesses, low energy, weight gain, eating more fatty and sugary foods, no interest in dressing nicely, skin pallor, excessive or insufficient sleeping, poor body care, member of the couch potato club, stomach distress, and shallow breathing.

Solutions - get off the couch and get on a daily exercise program, build a good diet by eating more fresh fruits and vegetables, limit sugar and fatty food, lower the caffeine, update the wardrobe, curb junk food, learn to breathe properly, go to bed and get up at regular times.

SOUL
Symptoms - when our inner source of life-energy droops, we become lethargic, distracted, unfulfilled, purposeless, withdrawn, self-absorbed, rudderless, without goals, disconnected, hopeless, and materialistic.

Solutions – meditate, practice yoga, pray, spend time in nature, take silent walks, learn relaxation techniques, join a community of those who share similar spiritual values, journal your daily reflections, attend a self-improvement seminar, read self-help books, see uplifting movies.

GUTS

Symptoms - feeling depressed, anxious, angry, guilty, confused, shame, imperfect, unworthy, rejected, lonely, unsuccessful, limited, lacking, sense of loss, disrespected, hopeless, cornered, out of time, powerless.

Solutions - learn to identify and handle feelings through individual and group counseling, find out how to accept and then work through emotions, share feelings with family and friends (most likely they have had some of the same feelings), learn how to appropriately express feelings.

THE BOTTOM LINES

Balance the "inner you." Identify the symptoms and solutions to strengthen, align and integrate the four quadrants of the inner business leader - Mind, Body, Soul and Guts. Add your combined business strengths. Be the powerful Whole Leader. Win big in business. Happily.

Lesson: 4

Three lessons for lasting leadership

Too much? Tired of reading long lists about how to be a leader? A better leader? An effective leader? But, think about the few, core characteristics that create lasting leaders. Not the job jumpers. But the leaders who stay and create sustainable successes. Who are they?

Simple searches will provide the lists of attributes associated with lasting leaders. You have read these lists – ad nauseam. The top ten articles in an Internet search produced more than two-dozen traits of successful leaders.

But the three most frequent characteristics of lifetime leaders are Honesty, Communications, and Positivity.

THE BEST POLICY

Honesty: this leadership quality is at the top of the list for real reasons:

- It breeds openness, trust, and human bonding.
- Honesty is at the root of good ethics.

- Telling the truth opens up two-way communications.
- Others will be honest, too.
- Customers will become more appreciative and loyal.
- Vendors will be better partners.
- Honesty means doing the right thing, no matter what.

Yet honesty does not mean that the leader has to tell everyone everything – that can create a new set of problems. Just tell the truth in all open communications.

Dishonesty breaks people, organizations, and businesses. Don't risk it. Ever.

LET'S GET TOGETHER

Communications: leaders who cannot communicate, cannot lead. And, the forms and forums of communications are many:

- Effective communications is two-way.
- The form can be in person, telephone, email, text, and videoconference.
- Good listening is a superior form of communications.
- Body language, tone of voice, and facial expression are communications.
- Let everyone involved know what is happening – avoid doubt and distrust.
- Share bad news before it happens, and good news as it happens.
- Communicating well means soliciting and receiving inputs.

And good leaders are sensitive to what is being communicated, to whom, why, where, when, and how. These set the critical context for communicating.

Obviously honesty reigns in all communications. That is the truth. Always.

ON THE HIGH ROAD

Positivity: no leader can get away with being downbeat, depressed, anxious, and withdrawn. Not for long. But an upbeat leader can work miracles:

- Employees, customers, vendors and other stakeholders become positive.
- Appropriately added humor helps build a more fluid and fun culture.
- Positivity helps overcome periodic disappointments with resiliency.
- Heavy workloads become less of an issue and more of a "can do" outlook.
- Teamwork is greatly accelerated and politics are diminished.
- Growth of the business is accelerated.
- Best employees are retained and new employees are attracted.

Positivity does not mean never being serious. Strong leaders must be appropriately serious while remaining positive overall.

But they are not Pollyanna's pretending that nothing is ever wrong. Never.

MORE ...

The top ten lists of great leader characteristics also include: delegation, confident, commitment, creative, intuitive, inspiring, empathy, consistency, flexible, conviction, respectful, resourceful, rewarding, knowledgeable, open to change, receptive, organized, initiative, responsible, accountable, courage, tenacity, patience, humility, visionary, ethical, visible, authentic, and many more.

Superhuman!

Point. The three must-have leadership qualities are: Honesty, Communications, and Positivity. Period.

A RECENT REVELATION

> "As we look ahead, leaders will be those who
> empower others."
>
> – BILL GATES

THE BOTTOM LINES

Three traits. These are the ones that build lifetime leaders. Yes there are many more characteristics of strong leaders. But three that are most often listed are Honesty, Communications, and Positivity. Master these three first. Then lead on.

Lesson: 5

Why high flying businesses stall in midair

Pilots know what CEO's should know - how to keep climbing without stalling and falling. What can put a good business into a tailspin, how can it be avoided, and how do we get out of one?

A good business might have taken off smoothly with strong leadership and staffing, innovative products and services, and some profitable growth. Everything is looking smooth, but the nice ride is hitting some turbulence.

Now what?

CAPTAIN NOT IN COMMAND

The leader of a growing business has let go of the controls. There is a weakening of the essential things that created a good business: vision, mission, values, strategy and execution. It is time to regenerate the business, strengthen it, and fly high again.

FLIGHT BOREDOM

Apathy, loss of passion, complacency and its deadly companion "there is no competition" are killers. Leaders must re-awaken the organization and themselves, instilling an energetic fresh sense of newness and excitement.

LISTLESS CREW

The once vibrant company can suffer from bad hiring practices and keeping poor performing employees too long. Reassess the organization and replace weak spots with great new people. Train and upgrade the team. Visibly reward the best performers.

STALE PEANUTS

Products and services have aged, not staying ahead of market needs. New product development and production are not in sync and too slow. Ensure constant teamwork among marketing, development and production. Get great new products to market, fast.

FLYING BLIND

There are no defined standards and no controls. Critical information is received too late. Set standards and periodically review them. Communicate expectations and track actual performance against standards. Report results and celebrate goal achievements.

POOR VISIBILITY

Marketing fails to understand and address a rapidly shifting market and customer base. Good products became positioned poorly against competition. Obtain current market trends, update marketing programs and make certain that sales plans are aligned.

UNHAPPY PASSENGERS
Customers receive little respect and get weak service. Their needs are not understood and met. Demand that the sales and service teams follow a proven process to care deeply for customers. It costs far less to keep a customer than to find a new one.

LOW FUEL
There is not enough cash via loans, investors, cash flow, and other means to sustain or accelerate growth. Implement a plan with resources to generate cash and investments. It is easier to do it before you need it, and keep plenty in reserve.

INSTRUMENT GLITCHES
Information technology may be outdated, too complex, and not best serve the organization. Manual procedures and training are misaligned with a good IT system. Dependency on IT is essential and must be continuously assessed and upgraded.

INFLEXIBLE FLIGHT PLAN
There is dogmatic adherence to what has worked to date, and failure to believe that constant change is mandatory. Always assess the entire business environment internally and externally, and make fast changes - holding to the vision for the business.

Clearly, it is time for the pilot of the business to do something, quickly.

Tom Zender

THE BOTTOM LINES
Grab the controls. Assess the business externally and internally, up-date the plan, make appropriate changes, recharge the organiza-tion, accelerate growth, and climb to sustainable success. Have a nice flight!

Lesson: 6

Why great leaders have "no" power

"**N**o!" We don't like to say it and we don't like to hear it. In childhood and today, in our I-want-it-now business culture, "no" can symbolize defeat. Yet, "no" is critical to success. Learn how to say "no" more often.

In a world of business driven by "yes" to ideas, prospects and customers, employees, and others, "no" seems contradictory to the ever-accelerating drive to rapid growth. Smart business leaders see otherwise.

WHY?
Saying "no" for the right reasons and in the right way is a primary way of staying focused, managing priorities and workloads, and simply saving money and time. We are not intending to dishonor nor harm those who want something from us, but we are intent upon being good leaders. Often the outcome is in the best interest of the requesters and the greater good of the organization. And, an appropriate "no" can amplify our decisiveness, authority,

strength, and respect. At best, do the right thing. Good leaders are not yes-men and yes-women.

HOW?

Because we like to please others, we are inclined to agree with them and say "yes," even when our intuition tells us otherwise. Take time to make the decision - it is too easy to commit to a hip-shot "yes." All "no's" can be professionally and politely delivered, along with our reasoning. Some "no's" can be unintentionally conditional (not now, not until, not yet), but be careful because these can be misinterpreted as a "yes." A better policy is an un-equivocal "no." We can change it later.

WHEN?

A good time to say "no" is as soon as possible (but only after we take time to think it over). A long-lingering decision can become an interpreted "yes" by default. The timing of telling one or more employees or others can depend upon business conditions, situations, events, and locale. If not right away, look for advanta-geous times in consideration of respect and empathy for every-one involved.

WHERE?

Often, our office or the recipient's offices are best to deliver a "no." Meetings on a face-to-face basis tell others that our deci-sion for a "no" is important. A good backup can be a visual/voice communication via today's Internet vehicles such as Skype, Go To Meeting and FaceTime - or a standard phone call. Leaving voice messages, texts and emails can work, depending upon the situ-ation. A written note or letter can be a personalized way to com-municate our decision.

WHO?

Usually, the leader, as an executive, manager, supervisor, committee head or a team point-person makes a "yes" or "no" decision and conveys it. And, in a more open environment we might circumstantially empower employees to say "no" to a request made of them.

Oh, and remember to sometimes say "no" to ourselves in a spirit of self-care, a lighter workload, and better work/life balance. Ahhhhh!

THE BOTTOM LINES

Just say "no." Understand the reasons for saying "no" and how to do it professionally and effectively in terms of when, where and who is involved. Get to know "no" for good business. Yes?

Lesson: 7

Know what to ask: great questions have great power

Potent questions fuel the engine of good business and sustainable success.

Honest answers to penetrating questions result in focused objectives, expanded opportunities and vibrant organizations. Below, are some well-focused questions to ask your organization – with individuals and in groups. Try these:

QUESTIONS ABOUT OBJECTIVES

What is the bigger problem we are attempting to solve? Too often we are dealing with less important issues.

Why? Why now? Understand the relative importance and timing of events.

What is the most important thing to accomplish today? Write this down on a highly visible note at the beginning of every day and complete it before anything else.

Can you get it done now? When we can do something important, do it right away.

What do you need to make it happen? This question creates a shared responsibility to provide the resources required for achieving a goal.

How can this be different? Avoid getting caught with no options in a difficult situation.

What is the next step (or what are the next steps)? A good way to keep things moving forward.

QUESTIONS ABOUT OPPORTUNITIES

What is the potential upside? What is the effort involved? What is the probability of success? What is the strategic value? Whenever there is a new opportunity, the answers to these questions are essential.

What are the risks and what would we do if they occur? What is the worst that could happen? Given that things can go wrong, identify them beforehand and determine what actions to take if they do misfire – including a decision to not go forward with insurmountable risks.

What problem are we solving? In meetings we often find ourselves having completely different conversations, so ask if we are working on the best opportunity.

What do you think? Asking others for their inputs is critical so that they can be heard and valued, and more often than not some useful ideas will emerge.

What else? A powerful question that can open up endless possibilities.

QUESTIONS ABOUT ORGANIZATION

What are our values? When we know them and think, speak and act according to them, we are more authentic and energetic.

How are you perceived that you do not know? Find out what others really think of you, good or bad, so that you can improve.

What can you do today to improve? Steady steps of improvement will achieve great things.

Will you be my mentor? When asked sincerely, almost nobody will turn you down – especially someone in a role and industry of interest to you.

What did you learn today? If we learned something new and valuable, it was a day worth having and remembering.

Who or what did you improve today? By knowing that we gave of ourselves, we can sum up our day at sundown and rest well.

A TIMELESS QUESTION

What are you pretending not to know? This question appeared decades ago. When we stop fooling ourselves and others new possibilities arise.

THE BOTTOM LINES

Start asking now. Build a list of favorite questions to use. Query individuals and groups with the questions that will help them and your overall organization. And, ask some key questions of yourself, frequently. Especially, what are you pretending not to know?

Lesson: 8

Why every company needs its own "Skunk Works" incubator

Need new products fast? Frustration among business leaders about time-to-market for new products is common. Speed counts in accelerating market demands. What can we learn from a bold move by Lockheed?

In the 1950's Lockheed was challenged by the Department of Defense to develop two advanced "it can't be done" aircraft. A respected aeronautical engineering manager, Kelly Johnson, ran the project with a select team, ample resources and an offsite facility that became known as the Skunk Works.

WHAT'S THE POINT?

This team quickly created the U-2 piloted reconnaissance aircraft, which first flew in 1955 at a record 70,000 feet. Then, they hatched the SR-71 Blackbird, an exotic titanium craft that first flew in 1964 and still holds world records for altitude at 80,000 feet and speed of 2,250 miles per hour. The U-2 and the SR-71 are still flown after 50 years.

We learned that highly focused teams that operate outside the normal business flow are most likely to produce "new wave" products that capture the minds and money of customers. This is now true of small, midsize and large companies.

HOW TO BUILD A GREAT INCUBATOR

In-house startup projects fly best when they have some well-orchestrated strengths:

Isolated facility - one of the keys to Lockheed's success, and many company incubators since, is the use of a completely separate physical place, isolated from the main facilities.

Sustained resources - incubator projects do not get delayed because their resources are never sidetracked for mainstream business needs. Don't tell the team what they are going to get - ask them what they need.

Winning team - startup projects are well staffed with the best talent, strongly funded and provided with proven, experienced team leadership.

Speed junkies - the incubator team has a natural bent to win the race against time in order to benefit the strategic interests of the company and its customers.

Sharp focus - the project is outlined with clear objectives, even when it is unclear about how some parts of the program can be done - or if they can be accomplished at all.

Top priority - skunk works projects, even when secret (which they often need to be), are given highest precedence when they are strategically critical to the business.

The Champion - a high level executive is assigned to move the incubation and production to completion while preserving the integrity of the team and its work.

INCUBATORS EVERYWHERE

Many corporations began in a garage or basement, and now continue with major offsite incubators of their own. They include: Google X, Boeing Phantom Works, Amazon Lab126, Apple Design Lab, DuPont Experimental Station, Ford Special Vehicle Team, Nike Innovation Kitchen, and the Nordstrom Innovation Lab. Create yours – even on a small scale.

THE BOTTOM LINES

Incubate something new. Even if a project only requires one or a few people, isolate them and give them the best resources, including their Champion. Set a very high priority with clear objectives, stay out of their way and let them deliver the magic. Get to work.

Lesson: 9

The five laws of laughter in leadership

Ever see or hear something at work and laughed yourself silly? Many of us need a good laugh because we are too often serious, stressed and scared about business. Yet, there are big benefits in lightening up the workplace. And, you do not need a clown suit!

We cannot be anxious and laugh in the same moment. A recent article in *Psychology Today* highlighted some benefits of laughter—it comforts us and combats fear, relaxes our body, minimizes stress and reduces pain—at home and at work. Create some humor.

BUSINESS LEADERS LISTEN UP

Laughter increases productivity, develops creativity, expands learning, strengthens relationships, builds teamwork, creates opportunities, prompts creativity and, yes, enhances leadership. Make it a practice to enjoy some laughter every day and spread some around your business—with peers, employees, customers and vendors. And yourself.

Forbes Magazine reported, "Tasteful humor is a key to success at work, but there's a good chance your co-workers aren't cracking jokes or packaging information with wit on a regular basis—and your office could probably stand to have a little more fun."

Outside the office, many of us have enjoyed for 25 years the daily cartoon, *Dilbert,* by Scott Adams. Most of us laugh at the wacky (and sometimes true) behaviors of leaders, managers and employees.

A SAMPLE OF SUCCESS

Southwest Airlines founder and first CEO, Herb Kelleher, built a company culture loved by his employees. He was known as the "clown prince" of the airlines, sometimes dressing up in crazy clothes and adding other antics just for fun. His employees followed by singing their humorous announcements to passengers—yet serious about doing their jobs well.

The company has been among the most admired American corporations, and Kelleher one of the best CEOs in *Fortune Magazine's* annual poll. The airline's camaraderie and friendliness is applauded. The bond between Kelleher and his employees helped give Southwest 23 consecutive years of profitability.

LAWS OF LAUGHTER
AT WORK

1. Humor is having fun in the workplace and chances are that if you think something is fun, other people will think so, too. Laughter is contagious and they will follow you.

2. Poke fun at yourself because it highlights your honesty and others will see it. And, they might add some additional laughter by poking fun at themselves.
3. Lightness can be incredibly versatile to improve most situations. Enjoy work more by adding some laughter each day.
4. Be professional. Don't embarrass others or put them down, and do use appropriate, clean humor. Fun can help just about everyone and doesn't always have to cause laughter—smiles work, too.
5. Encourage other people to use humor. Support them by smiling and laughing to let them know you appreciate their fun side.

THE BOTTOM LINES

Lighten up. Laugh at yourself and encourage humor in your organization. Be appropriate about using humor and others will follow. Watch your leadership and your organization become more creative and productive, and healthier in mind, body and spirit. Smile everyone!

Lesson: 10

Simplifiers vs. complicators: leadership uncluttered

"Great leaders are almost always great simplifiers."

– GEN. COLIN POWELL

Why does it take so long to get the new product to market? And, what is causing potential buyers to reject it when it appears? When will production finally be able to mass-produce it? How can anyone not understand the wonderful features of the new service offering? And, when will employees finally appreciate some of the benefits that are provided to them? The answer is simple.

Complexity is an overarching reason why so many things do not go according to plan. Sure, sometimes complexity is necessary, such as the inner workings of a computer. But, what the user sees needs to be clear, efficient, and ... simple.

COMPOUND COMPLEXITY

Unnecessary complication has several emotional roots. We might feel that for something to be good, it has to be complicated. Those who over complicate things might believe that they will be perceived as more intelligent, important, and professional. Not so.

If it takes excessively more time than necessary to create something, then someone's job preservation could be an ulterior motive. And, it might be more comfortable to keep working on an elongated project rather than taking on a new one.

Other contributors to inordinate complexity include:

- Lack of clarity about the objective of a project.
- Seeing too many possibilities and no priorities.
- No discussion about simplification in the planning.
- Not doing things in stages instead of all at once.
- Jumping to conclusions and solutions.

INTRODUCED INTRICACY

The Airbus 380, competitor to the Boeing 747 jumbo jet, was to be completed in 2006. But, it was two years late and overran the budget by $6 billion.

Excessive complexity was due to a multi-national design and implementation team, an overly intricate wiring system, a misaligned organization, and a hyper-aggressive schedule. While the A380 did fly, sales did not. Recent press suggests that the A380's long-term viability is a question.

STRAIGHT SIMPLICITY

When the value of simplicity becomes clear, focus will be placed on creating uncomplicated products, services, and processes. Good leaders will demand it and track it. They will simplify everything possible. Continuously.

Just because something is simple, does not mean that it must have limited functionality. It just needs to be easy to use by its intended audience. More functionality can be added in later, but will have an ease-of-use essence.

Simplicity has many benefits, including:
Better design – faster production
Easier demonstration – quicker sale
Cooler esthetics – greater attraction
Speedier education – rapid adaptation
Increased reliability – happier customers

UTTERLY UNCLUTTERED

Apple drove home the value of simple elegance: irresistible design; efficient user interface; dazzling demonstrations; rapid sales cycle; easy to install, learn, use, and upgrade; growing global market; feature rich; family of equally simple compatible devices (iPhone, iPad, iPod, iWatch); loyal customers.

Their revenues and profits continue to grow, their cash position is more than Microsoft's and Google's combined, and they are now the world's most valuable company. Beat that.

MISS AND KISS

Make it Super-Simple first, and then Keep it Super-Simple.

THE BOTTOM LINES

Un-complicate. Design and develop simplicity into products, services, and processes. Teach teams to go for the uncluttered. Don't introduce complexity. View things from the perspective of a user. Make it simple. Keep it simple.

Lesson: 11

Internal marketing: when employees are the market

Something is missing. When your marketing and public relations is focused only on pubic customers who believe and buy, there is a major missed opportunity. Yes, all that external marketing is critical to generating revenues and profits. But, marketing to the internal public is fundamental. Who are they?

Employees. They are another key audience, believing and buying into working for the organization. At least you hope so. Ignoring them is bad business and bad for business.

Repeated research demonstrates that when employees are viewed as another important audience, and marketed to as such, the company has a greater go at success. Very important.

HAPPY EMPLOYEES, HAPPY CUSTOMERS

Proof? For decades, Southwest Airlines has focused first on developing happy employees. The company leaders serve the employees (aka, "servant leaders)." The employees, with their feeling of wellbeing, go to long lengths to serve customers. Satisfied customers return repeatedly and their word-of-mouth spreads to new customers. From the beginning Southwest took off, expanded rapidly, and achieved high profits. They still do.

American Express research concluded that 78% of the buying public has stopped a purchase because of poor customer service. The offending employees were not willing or able to satisfy the buyer. The good news? This can be fixed.

Happy employees are more trainable and can be educated about how to create positive buying experiences and happy customers.

THE SACRED SAUCE

Good businesses, large and small, keep their employees "in the know." They share with their workforce, from top to bottom everywhere, the same information that is given to the public. This is easy and inexpensive with digital communications.

A few examples of the kinds of public marketing information that should be shared with all employees include:

- Press releases
- Product and service information
- Advertising (including audio/visual)
- Trade show attendance
- Significant customers
- Major orders
- New hires
- Customer endorsements

- Public news about the company, including significant events
- Selected financial information

These and other kinds of information keep employees informed and engaged. Some employers give the same simple and inexpensive gifts to employees as are given out at trade shows: shirts, pens, cups, note pads. A little means a lot.

PAYOFFS

Some of the benefits of internal marketing to employees are added trust, higher morale, sense of bonding and belonging, better employee retention, ease of training, and greater overall happiness.

Research by Northwestern University demonstrates that there is a definite link between internal marketing and profitability. The participating companies included Kellogg's, Cisco, The Container Store, 3M, McDonald's, Union Pacific, Chipotle Mexican Food, Staples, plus others.

Apple promotes its brand image by having their employees accurately represent that image. Anyone who has been to an Apple store knows that the employees are experts in the products they sell, and they are willing to answer an endless number of questions. These employees are smart, accessible, knowledgeable, and positively reflect the company. Apple employees are happy and upbeat. So are Apple customers.

THE BOTTOM LINES

Go inside. Yes, market externally as always, but remember your employees are an equally important market. Inform them as though they are customers and the press. Educate and market to them. Make them happy. They will make customers happy. You will be happy, too.

Lesson: 12

The company bus: on it, under it, or off it

Someone has been thrown under the bus; the company bus, synonymous for the organization. A once-valued company ally – an employee or a peer, board member, vendor, distributor – has been abruptly demoted or abandoned. They have been thrown under the bus, while survivors continue to be part of the organization. They are still on the bus.

The term "under the bus" started to appear as a popular term during the 2008 election. When a political friend or supporter was viewed as a deterrent, a candidate might let go of them for personal gain. The former friend was thrown under the political bus for the remainder of the campaign.

ON THE BUS
The riders are those in good stead with the leader's organization. They are viewed as good employees and other allies, and valuable to the purpose of the company.

So, the organization continues to move forward and these riders are feeling secure in their positions with their seat belts fastened. They continue to work in good faith and enjoy working in a great situation. They stay on the bus and are happy riders. Maybe.

UNDER THE BUS

Trouble. The bus is blowing smoke, overheating, and the shock absorbers are gone. The ride has turned rough. Weak leadership has taken its toll. Without warning, some of the people on the bus are expendable and are terminated. They have been thrown under the bus. Painful.

Yes, there will be a reason: "rationalized workforce" (layoff), declining revenues and profits, poor performance (often not the employee, but the company leadership), and reorganization. More pain.

Of course, sometimes changes in an organization are truly necessary, in spite of good leadership. The truth is that some employees are poor performers. But, in today's corporate lingo, even these people have been thrown under the bus.

OFF THE BUS

> "There are three constants in life ... change, choice, and principles."
>
> – STEPHEN COVEY.

When the organizational bus is no longer productive or purposeful there are some options:

- Stay on the bus – do our best, and see what happens.
- Change seats – look for a better situation in the company.

- Suggest to the leader-driver a different road – a new strategy.
- Head for a rest stop – take some time off and think it over.
- Fill up with a better grade of fuel – re-energize with good self-care.
- Wash the windshield – see things with a new perspective.
- Have a talk with the driver – discuss the situation with the leader.

Perhaps it is time to leave the bus, particularly if there are repeated warning lights that you are a likely candidate to be thrown under the bus.

If you decide to get off the bus, start looking for a new bus. One that has a great leader, powerful purpose, clear vision, motivating mission, and one where your talents are in gear with their needs.

THE BOTTOM LINES

Check your bus. Are you happy with your organization and your role in it – riding on the bus? Or, do you have a doom-sense that you will be asked to leave the organization – to be thrown under the bus? Choose: stay on the bus, risk getting thrown under the bus, or look for a better bus. Bus stop coming up.

Lesson: 13

The five stages of employee-employer bonding

New job? The employee is excited about it. They have feelings of perfection, a bit of a high, on a pink cloud. The employer might feel the same way. They have found the perfect employee, a great productive star. Euphoria!

But, because this is a human relationship, this "honeymoon" stage likely will not last. Reality sets in, things change, and both employee and employer do not meet some expectations. What's wrong?

Normally nothing. Like all relationships, this one is moving through five stages of change: Engagement, Reality, Stability, Commitment, and Growth.

ENGAGEMENT

The new employee has been through the job search and has found a great possibility. And, the employer has been looking for the perfect person to fill a much-needed position.

The job starts, introductions are made, and the assignment begins. The new employee and the employer see only the up-side. Endorphins are Hollywood-high. The employee completes the first assignment perfectly. All is well.

May this stage never end. But it does. Something is changing. Sigh.

REALITY

Ooops. The employee makes a mistake. The employer reacts. Differences show up. The employee feels that they are right – so does the employer. Conflict.

Another mistake occurs. This time the employer blew it. The employee feels offended. There are no harsh words, they ride over the bump, but now both are emotionally on guard. The process continues.

At some point the employee wonders if they made a mistake in joining the organization – and the employer is asking themselves if they made a bad hire. This is when a divorce most likely can occur. But, things can get better.

STABILITY

Acceptance is the turning point. Mutual acceptance. As long as the employee does not commit a "fatal error" – and shows overall strength – progress is made.

Both the employer and the employee accept each other's strengths and weaknesses. They learn to work together. In fact, their strengths and weaknesses might complement each other.

They have found their way and the employee is viewed as a strong overall contributor. The employee respects the employer and gives their best to the organization. Peace reigns and performance gains.

COMMITMENT

The employee connects more deeply with the organization and decides to make it their permanent home. They surrender to the give-and-take of the business. They feel that they are now truly part of a family.

And, the employer now has the benefit of a good, trustworthy, committed employee. Doubt slips away and the employer can count on the employee.

A sense of belonging enhances the employee's performance. They want to work in the organization on a long-term basis for their career. There is a degree of safety. Whew!

COLLABORATION

In time, the employer and employee find additional opportunities to expand their relationship for the good of the organization. There is a high degree of success.

The employer finds promotional possibilities, broader responsibilities, and offers them to the employee. The employee happily accepts and keeps expanding.

They both learn that moving through these five stages of an employee-employer relationship benefits them, the organization, and ultimately customers of the business. Win-win-win.

THE BOTTOM LINES

No robots. Human relationships are the core of organizations. Just as in personal relationships, there are five stages to creating good workplace relationships. Understand them and build strong teams. People bond. Robots do not.

Lesson: 14

Drama, trauma, and the dysfunctional business family

No, not family business. Business family. Most business orga- nizations behave like a family in some way. If a household family is dysfunctional, they are not operating in unison. Blowups occur. If a business organization is dysfunctional, the business blows up. Stop it soon.

Amazing. Estimates state that 35% to 70% of American fami- lies are dysfunctional. When these people become part of our workforce, they carry their behavioral baggage with them.

And, the costs are high in family life and business life – in both human and financial capital. Read on.

PARENTS, KIDS, RELATIVES, AND OH MY

Before we look at issues with our employees (our organizational family), let's first understand the dysfunctional at home family. Here are a few core characteristics:

Unstated rules – they are vague and changing; "we don't have any problems"; don't tell so-and-so; feelings don't matter, just appearances and performance.

Perfectionism – constant criticism can leave kids feeling worthlessness. Later, they may criticize themselves and others – and may fear success or failure.

Communication – needs and feelings are not expressed directly; "Do me a favor" translates to "Do it now or else"; bad behaviors are rationalized.

Triangulation –using one family member as a go-between, instead of speaking directly to someone; this becomes "normal," yet it is twisted.

Rigidity – there is only one correct way to be or act; don't be spontaneous; don't have fun, don't relax; don't be yourself.

Blame – dysfunctional families indict each other; errors are corrected harshly; shame and blame are heaped on; ducking responsibility; overreaction.

Shame – family members are negatively compared and judged; name calling; overly high standards set a stage for failure; no one is ever good enough.

Once these ways of life become deeply embedded, they are carried over into careers, jobs, and work. Big problem.

DYSFUNCTIONAL DISEASE

Every organization will have some level of dysfunctional behaviors. Sometimes widespread, and sometimes within a group. Both are bad.

If the leader is dysfunctional, the rest of the organization will tend to follow. If a group leader is the root, the group rots. Even if a key employee's dysfunction is sΩtrong, that person will be a potential carrier of the behavioral disorder to others.

The costs are high: lost momentum and motivation, financial drains, poor quality, lost time, rework, and loss of good people. The dysfunctional people will tend to stay. They have found a familiar home. You must fix things fast.

CLEAN UP THE HOUSE

No, do not fire everyone. Using internal and external HR resources, develop a plan and actions to mitigate and eliminate bad behaviors. Here are some key ideas and actions:

1. Hold a series of meetings to educate and discuss dysfunctional behaviors.
2. Do not single out specific people in public (yes, privately when necessary).
3. Have all leaders involved in these meetings.
4. Point out the cost of dysfunctional behaviors.
5. Offer incentives to move from dysfunctional to functional behaviors.
6. Provide internal or external counseling to help individuals.

7. Keep going with an ongoing program of brief weekly meetings.

This process can include a professional expert to describe how household family dynamics influence workplace behaviors, the costs, and the benefits of change.

THE BOTTOM LINES

Identify organizational dysfunction. Translate household behaviors to workplace behaviors. Educate everyone about the costs. Hold ongoing discussions with groups and individuals. Incent people to change. No blame, no shame. Just gain.

Lesson: 15

Mission, vision, and (huh?) purpose

The idea of "mission" is a concept born in the military – what to do in a competitive setting. In business the mission describes what a company does and for whom. More recently, "vision" became an overriding statement of what the business will look like in the future. But few ask the key question: why does the business exist?

Mission: an example of a clear mission statement is, "Apple is committed to bringing the best personal computing experience to students, educators, creative professionals and consumers around the world through its innovative hardware, software and Internet offerings." This describes clearly what the company does and for whom.

Vision: Mattel's vision statement simply states what the company wants to become, "To be the premier toy brand – today and tomorrow." This is an internal view of what they want to be across time.

THE MISSING PIECE

Purpose: why does this company exist? What is it doing for the world? What is its cause? Why should anyone care about this business? What does the organization believe in, stand for, and live up to?

A solid purpose is born out of the answers to the above questions. Purpose sets the grand cause of the company. A higher purpose attracts customers, employees, and other stakeholders. It is a motivating force. A constant compass.

We like to purchase products and services from companies who do things to improve our world. We feel good about doing business with them.

PURPOSEFUL EXAMPLES

Here are some powerful purpose statements from well-known businesses:

Hilton Worldwide – "fill the earth with the light and warmth of hospitality."

McGraw-Hill Companies – "creating economic growth, job creation, and a smarter, better world."

DuPont Corporation – "creating sustainable essentials to a better, safer, and healthier life for people."

Johnson & Johnson – "caring for the world, one person at a time."

Nintendo – "to put smiles on the faces of everyone we touch."

General Electric – "GE people worldwide are dedicated to turning imaginative ideas into leading products and services that help solve some of the world's toughest problems."

Nike – "bring inspiration and innovation to every athlete in the world."

BUY FEELINGS

Most leaders and employees think in a two-step sequence (including in a sales situation): what - how. Example:

"We have the best widget (what), and it is intelligently intuitive (how) - would you like to buy one?"

"Not really (ho-hum)."

Lead with "why." In a reversed inside-out process, great leaders and their teams form a business proposition in three-steps: why-how-what. Example:

"We smash rules in every great thing we do (why); we design intelligent intuitiveness into all our products (how); we provide wonderful widgets (what)."

"Would you like to purchase one?"

"Yes (exciting)."

"By the way, we have some other widgets, too - would you like to see them?"

"Of course!"

THE BOTTOM LINES

Begin with purpose. Why does this business exist in a worldview? Build mission and vision around purpose. It is a constant compass for the company. Drive thoughts, words, and actions via the inside-out flow of "why, how, what." Attract customers, employees, and stakeholders. End with profits.

Lesson: 16

The one-word strategy

Why make it so complicated? Strategy sounds difficult. Sometimes it is - but only as complex as we make it. In most cases, a single word can define the overall direction of an organization (or individual). Strategy is the guidepost in choosing what to do and making decisions in an environment that has limited resources. Sure, having a more broadly defined strategy may be appropriate and necessary. But, start simply. One word.

"THE GODFATHER"

Francis Ford Cappola, film director and producer and winner of multiple Academy Award Oscar's, including *The Godfather*, has a one word strategy for each of his movies. Cappola notes, *"Every time I made a film, I always knew what I thought the strategy was, the core, in one word. In 'The Godfather,' it was succession. In 'The Conversation,' it was privacy. In 'Apocalypse,' it was morality."*

His reasoning is that it helps him to make a myriad of monumental and minute decisions. In most cases, he refers to his one word strategy for the movie to help with his choices. An example is that his movie *"The Conversation"* he needed to make a choice about a raincoat for one of the actors. His one word strategy for the movie was "privacy." He paradoxically chose a clear plastic raincoat for effect.

ONE-WORD ORGANIZATIONS

The one-word strategy can be a guide for successful organizations. Mike Smith, coach of the Atlanta Falcons, chose the word "finish." It inspired his team to always finish strong. Why? The right word provides lucidity, focus, energy, and excitement to propel individuals and organizations to great success. While an organizational or individual goal might fizzle, a strong one-word strategy attracts and inspires higher planes of performance.

IBM founder Thomas Watson coined an infamous word at the start of the company to focus the company, its employees, and even customers to rise up into new realms of possibilities. The word is "Think." It has been displayed in many different ways: on walls, on desk plaques, and on shirts. Has is worked? Every year, IBM is issued more United States patents than any other company, worldwide.

Here is a short list of one-word strategies across time from a number of companies:

- 3M - *Innovation*
- HP - *Invent*
- IBM - *Think*
- NEXTEL - *Done*
- Rover - *Relax*
- Samsung - *Imagine*
- United Airlines - *Rising*

- Capella University - *Matter*
- Kaiser Permanente - *Thrive*
- Acura - *Advance*
- Budweiser - *True*
- Nissan - *Driven*

An interesting twist is that Apple has a competitive two-word version of IBM's *Think* – it is *Think Differently.*

THE STRONG AND
THE WEAK

Strong one-word strategies have key attributes:
Memorable, recall a positive emotion, have a benefit, unique, believable, simple, provocative, original, acceptable.

Weak one-word strategies have negative characteristics:
Clumsy, complicated, meaningless, boring, contestable, negative, pretentious, combative, irritating, bland, used by others.

"Why need I volumes, if one word suffice."

– RALPH WALDO EMERSON

THE BOTTOM LINES

Short. Find a company, organizational, or individual one-word strategy. Ask employees, ask yourself, group think. What one word best captures the essential clarity, focus, energy, and excitement needed – and fulcrum for making decisions? Seek and search until you find it. Simple.

Lesson: 17

The leader's wall: through it, over it, under it, around it

No, this is not the wall where leaders, managers, and individuals hang their awards of achievement. This is the wall of challenge, confusion, and chaos. A seemingly insurmountable problem is in the way of progress. You are up against the wall. But, do not give up. Get beyond the wall.

Time to get the team together and brainstorm one or more strategies to face the wall and do something extraordinary. If you ignore it, a thicker wall might stop your business.

Don't beat your head against the wall. Below, are some strategic options.

THROUGH THE WALL
Breaking through the problem with creative thinking by your team is a possible solution. Brainstorm a battering ram of an idea to overcome the challenge.

If the problem is less severe than originally anticipated, it might be possible to simply move through the wall as though it is wallpaper.

Example: Faced with competition from Microsoft and conventional PC's, Apple adopted Intel-compatible chips, licensed Microsoft's Office suite, launched compatible mobile devices (iPhone, iPod, iPad), used sleek product designs, upped its marketing muscle, and introduced Apple retail stores. Today, Apple is one of the world's most valuable companies. Microsoft isn't.

OVER THE WALL

Think at a higher level. What flight of a fantastic idea would lift the organization beyond the challenge it faces?

Einstein said, "We cannot solve a problem with the same mind we used when we created the problem." Ergo, think beyond the box.

Example: Lockheed developed an advanced "it can't be done" aircraft. An isolated team with ample resources and a great leader quickly created the SR-71 Blackbird, an exotic titanium craft that first flew in 1964. It still holds records for piloted production aircraft with an altitude at 80,000+ feet and speed of 2,250+ miles per hour.

UNDER THE WALL

Dig deeper for a solution. Find ways to undermine the threat. Sometimes a surprise move will upset the status quo and allow you to sneak under the problem.

History is filled with demonstrations of how people and devices succeeded by getting beneath the problem. Tunnels, submarines, and radar-evading aircraft are a few samples.

Example: Sales of the popular pain reliever Excedrin were dropping with conventional marketing. This market is a crowded one with established and new players. Excedrin devised an underground marketing program. Sales turned around and took off again within 12 months.

AROUND THE WALL

Deceptively go around the wall of resistance. Use an end-run path of least resistance.

How to do this? An out-of-context idea can allow a spontaneous solution to emerge.

Example: Ericsson pioneered a cellphone with a digital camera. Marketing struggled with traditional ways to excite customers. So, they used 60 actors in major cities that posed as tourists, asking strangers to take their picture. The strangers were handed the new cell/camera, along with an enthusiastic education about how to use it. Afterward, the strangers talked up their experience with others. Sales took off around the wall. Hello, viral marketing.

THE BOTTOM LINES

See the wall. Understand the barriers to progress with any part of the organization – sales, marketing, product, or other. Use your team to find ways through, over, under, or around any walls of challenge, confusion, or chaos. Don't stop. Get past the wall.

Lesson: 18

Three invisible business tools: insight, intuition and innovation

Innovation is the engine of business. It generates novel ideas, never before products and new services that scoop new revenues into the sales streams of business.

ABOUT INNOVATION
Aristotle and Plato argued that our brain is a physical thinking mechanism and that our mind a function of our inner being. Quantum physics suggests that the energy of our inner creative ideas flow into our minds 10,000 times faster than the speed of light –– in virtually "no time."

Regardless of the Greeks and scientists, we have many names for this phenomenon: an "aha moment," from "out of the blue" and the "creative nudge."

WHAT ABOUT INTUITION
AND INSIGHT?

Insight is suddenly seeing something that was already there, sometimes abruptly -- an involuntary collision of seemingly disparate information which we already have. Malcolm Forbes noted that his best vision was insight.

Intuition is a sudden realization or comprehension of the essence or meaning of something. It's as though we have found the last "piece of the puzzle" and are now seeing the entire picture. Albert Einstein said that he relied upon intuition in his innovative work.

Insight and intuition fuel innovation. The more we expand our insight and intuition, the more likely we are to be innovative.

BEING AN INNOVATOR

As children most of us were naturally innovative. But, for many this native creativity became suppressed as our lives progressed.

So, is there something we can do to recover our natural innovation?

The idea of "clearing our desk" and "shutting our door" so that we can better focus on something important is a common practice. We can let go of our mental and physical business and take a constructive break. This provides an environment in which new ideas can better emerge.

RELAXATION IS KEY

Many agree that an inner calm boosts creativity. The benefits of unwinding include amplified access to insight and intuition, less stress and more freedom to innovate, and a sharper focus on giving shape to new ideas.

The methods of relaxation are very individualized: sit or lie down comfortably in silence, take a walk in a quiet beautiful place, practice a calming form of yoga, or listen to soft sounds.

Meditation is increasingly popular as a relaxation technique. There are many forms to choose from and most are easy to learn.

Steve Jobs, the creative founder of Apple, was a long time meditator. The executives of Google adopted meditation within their first 100 employees and now offer meditation courses and quiet rooms to all their 30,000 worldwide employees. Both companies are among the world's most innovative and successful.

THE BOTTOM LINES

Take time out. Find a form of relaxation that works and practice it daily – or multiple times per day – on a consistent basis. Note new insights and intuitions. Birth more innovation. Grab the great ideas. Innovate. Put them to work. Literally.

Lesson: 19

The new yoga of leadership flexibility

Feeling adrift in a business world where uncertainty is the norm? Where complex problems bubble up quickly and defy conventional leadership thinking?

Past polls by business media and university business schools typically listed confidence, communications, commitment and creativity as top leadership qualities. Yet, in our spiraling world of change, most of those polls did not list flexibility.

Then, the digital revolution exploded, leadership transcended management, business cycles sped into a blur, and flexible leadership sprung up.

WHAT IS IT?
Scott Yorkovich, a Capella University adjunct faculty member, defines flexible leadership as, *"the ability to receive and process diverse and potentially conflicting sources of information, the openness to implement a variety of strategic solutions, and the ability to adapt to changing conditions."*

What flexible leadership is not: not saying "yes" to everything everyone asks for; not just about flexible hours and workplaces; not being all things to all people inside and outside the organization. Good flexible leadership demands good management to achieve it.

WHY DO IT?

The benefits of leadership flexibility easily outweigh the time it takes to learn how and start practicing it:

Turn on a dime - adapt to (or cause) rapid change in the mad race of the marketplace.

Mitigate excessive structure - too many rules and regulations stifle flexibility.

Minimize reactiveness - creatively respond to changes in time rather than chaotically reacting too late.

Strengthen the organization - creates more of an adaptive atmosphere, a more interesting place to work, a fun environment that attracts and retains employees.

Examples of flexible leadership in action:

- Bank of America for early adoption of Internet banking in spite of safety concerns.
- Wal-Mart for building an IT infrastructure before the business took off.
- Toyota for perfecting the hybrid vehicle with Prius when cars were gas only.

HOW DO IT?

To become a more flexible leader the first step is being flexible about becoming flexible. Here are some key practices to get started:

Think of "we," not "me" - check the ego at the front door and embrace some flexibility for the overall good of the organization and the business.

Listen carefully - encourage others to offer valuable ideas about anything so that the entire team becomes a true participant in the business.

Keep key principles and values in place - but vary processes and problem solving dynamically.

Shoot for "what" rather than "how" - give people the room to accomplish things well and on-time in a way that works best for them.

More examples of companies with flexible leadership:

- Apple Computer for flexible software and systems while adhering to design principles.
- Southwest Airlines for adaptive job roles, yet holding the principle of one type of aircraft.
- Berkshire-Hathaway for investing in many industries, but staying with the principal of value.

THE BOTTOM LINES

Stretch out. Pick at least one technique to become more flexible. Learn when to apply flexibility and when not to. Put it into practice in an area or two and then grow from there. Consciously manage flexibility. It's healthy for business.

Lesson: 20

Be a bold business leader: step out of anxiety and into action

To start something new, start something new. Seems simple. Yet, why do so many leaders and others fail to initiate new actions in our ASAP business world? Learn how to stop waiting and start moving.

Organizations can be topped out with great visions, missions, values, intentions, goals, and plans. But, until action is initiated everything else is nothing but smoke.

WHAT HOLDS US BACK?
Fear is usually the parking brake on the first step toward success. Human behavior experts have given us key reasons for why we freeze in fear instead of taking action:

Fear of failure - some of us don't act because we do not want to be blamed for something that does not work out as expected.

Fear of success - if we feel unworthy or undeserving, then staying behind is safer than being recognized as a hero.

Fear of uncertainty - if we cannot be certain of what will happen, we will not take the risk of beginning.

Fear of change - oh yes, "we don't know how to do this," or "we have never done this before," or "it won't make any difference" - ergo, it is safer to stay put.

Fear of imperfection - if we lack some small resource, we continuously play out the game of "not ready yet," but the competitive clock is running.

These debilitating anxieties close the gates of opportunity and shut out the excitement of achieving greatness.

HOW CAN WE BYPASS FEAR AND GET MOVING?

Quotes about taking action in spite of fear include: "The only thing we have to fear is fear itself." - Franklin D. Roosevelt; "Jump, and you will find out how to unfold your wings as you fall." - Ray Bradbury; "Whatever you can do, or dream you can, begin it. Boldness has genius, power, and magic in it." - W. H. Murray.

- Don't wait for excessive data and analysis. General Colin Powell took action when he had 40% to 70% of the facts.
- Trust your intuition. Do some research, but avoid paralysis by analysis. Reasonably review things in order to be informed - and then go with your guts.
- Visualize achieving the goal in your mind. Do it daily and add feelings of excitement and success. This action helps you start the first step and take subsequent steps toward the goal.

- Up the energy. The closer to the goal we get, the more excitement we feel and the more energy we apply to getting across the finish line.
- Fail fast. Yes, some things are not going to work out. When that becomes apparent, stop and then start something else with a high priority. Eliminate thoughts of further failure.

Paradoxically, we can override fear by simply moving through it into action.

THE BOTTOM LINES

Step over fear. When you have enough information, intuition, vision and boldness, lead with the first step. Providence then steps in to help. Keep asking, "What is the next step?" and take it. See the goal being reached – until it is. Success trumps fear.

Lesson: 21

WIFT: when value delivered is not value perceived

What's in it For Them? You have delivered great value to your customers and exceeded their expectations. Surprisingly, they might not really know that. So, it is critical that you tell customers frequently about all the value you are delivering. This builds better business.

WHAT IS VALUE, ANYWAY?
The word "value" is spoken often, but few understand it. Value is in the mind's eye of the buyer and is a composite of many factors.

The common components of good value include: a pleasant atmosphere in which to conduct business, friendly transactions, trust and respect for buyer and seller, a good selection of products and services, convenience - all part of overall high quality.

Price? Gucci said it well, "Quality will be remembered long after price has been forgotten."

VALUE ON NOTICE

You received the orders, and you delivered with excellent value. Your customers paid your invoices, and you don't hear too much from them. You continue to do business together, month after month. All seems well.

Then, a shift hits the fan. A major customer has gone quiet, their complaints begin to appear, and their order rate begins to soften. What happened?

"NOTHING" HAPPENED

You likely are not informing customer management about the great value you are delivering. Yes, your invoice states what you provided, but only quantity and price - just part of overall value. And, perhaps just the customer's accounting department sees your invoice.

So, there may be little real understanding by your customers' management of your full value delivered. Worse, for lack of any positive perception, they could have a negative perception. What to do?

TELL ALL, SELL ALL

Here are ideas for letting customers know about the excellent value you are providing:

Spell out your value - draft a brief monthly message to each customer that outlines all of the value components you are delivering, not just price and quantity. For example, "We delivered in less than our agreed time, all 100 boxes that you ordered, for $500 under our quote, with no errors, and we provided three extra boxes at no charge. Thank you for your ongoing business!"

Communicate your value messages - to your customers' management, who authorize and send business to you. Send your value-delivered message by email or letter, or have your sales person hand deliver it.

Add your value to invoices - put the same value messages in front of your customers' accounts payable people who pay you. Include a big "Thank You!"

A SATISFYING EXAMPLE
Kroger is the largest grocery retailer in the United States, including its Fry's stores in Arizona. When checking out of Fry's, we are given direct and delighting reminders of value:

- We are asked, "Is everything OK?"
- They say, "You saved $X by shopping with us" (also printed on the receipt).
- We read on the receipt that we have received free fuel points - more savings when we purchase gasoline.
- Then we hear a clear, "Thank you!"

We leave knowing clearly what value we have received. We become loyal customers.

THE BOTTOM LINES
Declare your value. Let customers know about all your value delivered - not just price. Tell those who authorize and place orders with you, frequently. State your complete value on invoices and add, "Thank you!" Create customer loyalty.

Lesson: 22

When the CEO is not the leader, who is?

A ssumption: the CEO is always a leader. Fact: this is not always true. There are leaders who are not the CEO. Some CEO's want others to be the leaders in their organization. And, there are CEO's who pretend to be a leader - but are not. What gives?

WHAT IS A CEO, REALLY?

The Chief Executive Officer is the top-level senior officer in a business entity. They optimize the worth of a business in the midst of many variables and continuous change. CEO's balance resources and achieve objectives. They establish a forum for customers, employees and others to conduct business.

However, they are not always a leader, even if they are effective in their CEO role.

MYTHS ABOUT LEADERS

Leaders influence others to willingly participate in the attainment of a common objective. Followers of these leaders often do not report to the leader in a formal way, but work in a symbiotic relationship.

But, leadership has nothing to do with a number of factors, including:

Management - it is not the same as leadership. CEO's and other managers are meant to be the master mechanics of business, such as planning, overseeing, measuring, hiring, coordinating and more. But, leaders guide people, not things.

Personality - not all leaders are hard-charging extroverts who ooze charisma. Some may be born with built-in leadership qualities, but most have learned how to lead.

Rank and title - leaders may or may not be the highest-level executives, and vice-versa. And, pay grade does not automatically make a leader. Leadership qualities do.

Real leaders do not micro-manage, take credit for others' work nor diminish the self-esteem of people.

WILL THE REAL LEADERS PLEASE STAND UP?

Surveys about the common characteristics of strong leaders typically find the following:

TRUTHFULNESS

The honesty of a leader sets the standard for others to follow. In fact, integrity is an irresistible attraction to those who are willing to follow a good leader - whether they report to that leader or not.

INSPIRATION
Leaders paint a vision for the organization and effectively engage others to follow the vision - and to help attain it. Leaders keep morale high, literally as cheerleaders. Then, they visibly reward the active team members.

INTERACTION
Being able to clearly and appropriately articulate plans, actions and results with a team is key to successful leadership. Trust, openness, willingness to listen and ongoing interaction build and retain winning followers.

LIGHTNESS
Laughter increases productivity, develops creativity, expands learning, strengthens relationships, builds teamwork, creates opportunities, prompts creativity and, yes, enhances leadership.

DELEGATION
Leaders spot the strengths of others and then engage those people as willing participants in a great team. This frees the wise leader to address higher-level opportunities. The team and its members feel trusted.

Additional qualities of leadership include conviction, setting examples, being positive, creativity and intuition.

Yes, there are great CEO's who also are great leaders. But, beware of the self-proclaimed leader who is not. Know the difference.

THE BOTTOM LINES

Learn leadership. Whether you are a CEO or not, adopt the best qualities of good leaders and then put these attributes to work for your team. Foster and support other leaders in your organization. Do not fake leadership because you cannot. Others will know.

Lesson: 23

How to deal with happy customers

We have worked diligently to satisfy as many customers as possible. Why spend additional time with them when they are already in our camp? We may know how to manage unhappy customers, but we miss big opportunities when we do not manage our happy customers. Why?

It is normally easier and less expensive to keep existing customers, particularly very satisfied ones. We already know them and they know us - we have established relationships that work.

Expand these partnerships.

TIPS FOR MANAGING HAPPY CUSTOMERS

Make as many new customers happy from the very start, and keep them that way. Once they are completely satisfied, stay focused on keeping them happy. And even happier.

- They likely have not purchased all of the products and services we offer - and they might not know about our complete offerings. Tell them.
- We have established lines of communications with their organization. Keep them open.
- They must not feel that we are apathetic or uninterested, or more focused on selling to new prospects. Give them attention.
- Thank them often and appreciate them in every appropriate way. Be grateful.
- Find out what is making them happy and then give them more of it if possible. What would make them even more satisfied? Ask them.
- Don't put second tier teams in charge of the happiest customers because it is risky. Assign top teams.
- Keep telling your customers how much value you are delivering to them. Keep competition out.
- Make your happy smaller accounts even happier, too. Many of them will grow substantially over time and provide you with an expanding revenue stream. Grow with them.
- Give them something extra that they were not expecting – an additional product or service that will help them. No strings attached.
- Always be available to meet their needs with timely and appropriate responsiveness. Doing so is much easier than fixing festering issues. Frequently ask them if there are any concerns that should be addressed. Prevent problems.
- Listen to multiple members of the customer organization. Just because one customer person expresses happiness

with your company, does not mean all the customer people think the same. Take their pulse.

- Foster a culture of customer care. Recognize and reward your teams that support the happiest accounts. Customers first.
- Take a sign of appreciation to meetings with your good customers. Having something to eat is almost always good. Break bread together. Celebrate together when appropriate.
- Hold "happy customers" meetings with members of your organization to generate more ideas about how to best satisfy customers. Every idea counts.

NOT AT ALL COSTS

Stay in budget and keep your profit margins at appropriate levels. Don't give everything away.

The customer is not always right. Sometimes you need to find a win-win state of satisfaction, which will lead to increased happiness. Negotiate, don't capitulate.

When a given customer cannot be satisfied in any way, consider reducing support and spend more time with your better customers. Don't waste resources.

THE BOTTOM LINES

Keep customers happy. It costs far less than finding new ones. Make them even happier by an active program of increasing customer satisfaction. Find out what is making them happy and what else they would like. Don't cut your profitability – add to it. Keep happy customers.

Lesson: 24

Discover the power of consciousness in your business

Described as being aware something within oneself, consciousness is rising as an essential business component. Long the ground of philosophers, consciousness in business is capturing the minds of some CEO's. It may be the next higher ground of better businesses. It is coming into view.

In fact, the CEO's of major companies such as Whole Foods, Container Store, Trader Joe's and others have formed a nonprofit organization named Conscious Capitalism. It promotes higher levels of consciousness in business - voluntary exchange, entrepreneurship, competition, freedom to trade, trust, compassion, collaboration and value creation.

Call it conscious commerce or business consciousness; it aims to serve the best interests of customers, employees, owners, vendors, the community and others.

SO WHAT?
The hard hierarchy of commerce is evolving into a higher state of being in business. The lower levels of frightening, disappointing, antagonistic or demanding environments are ascending to higher levels of hopeful, harmonious, meaningful business.

Watch out, Maslow, we are taking the express elevator up your pyramid from the ground floor of survival to the self-actualized penthouse of well being for all stakeholders.

THE MARKERS OF
THE MOVEMENT
As this trend rides the rails of acceleration, inertia and momentum, there are some indicators of this millennial movement underway:

Information Age morphs into the Age of Consciousness, where big fairness and service to customers, employees and others is more important than big data.

Altruism ascends and "we" supersedes "me." The newest Gens already see their world this way. They are global and more interested in humanity than the next dollar.

Integrative awareness transcends dualistic thinking. Dualism says, "Either-or, black or white, only one way." Integration says, "Both-and, black and white, many ways." Great leaders can see infinite shades of options.

"Believing is seeing" surpasses "seeing is believing." Envisioning the future and painting our dreams in our minds with

positive feelings manifests surprising results. Great athletes do it. Great leaders are on to it.

English eclipses multiple tongues as the language of business. This began when American business powered worldwide commerce in post-WWII. The U.S. dominance of the Internet has amplified the sound of English in business. Global bonding at work.

Global business dominates local and national commerce. This was happening with early computers and communications, and the Internet has only accelerated it. We can see and hear our customer anywhere, anytime. We are wired to help each other.

Collaborative leadership trumps vertical management. Collaboration with prospects, customers, employees, vendors, the community, even appropriate cooperation with competitors, "coopetition." More people are swept into success.

Strategy and tactics blend, dynamically intertwined at all times. Strategy no longer drives actions – they flow together. Time shrinks and good business expands.

Humanity and the Internet intermesh and raise business consciousness. It becomes easier to spread compassionate collaboration in commerce - and more difficult to cheat.

Making life overrides making money - visionary leaders build companies with the purpose of building a good world that works for more people. They generate good profits in the process. They feel good, too.

Perhaps there is an acknowledgement that there is a spiritual aspect to conscious business. George Washington called it, "Providence."

THE BOTTOM LINES
Raise your business consciousness. Seek the tenets of conscious capitalism, including entrepreneurship, competition, fairness, trust, compassion, collaboration, and value creation - human and material. Participate in the movement to conscious commerce. Be aware.

Lesson: 25

The worst competition is internal competition

Think of your toughest competitor that keeps you awake at night. Now multiply it by several times. This is the internal competition of rivalry among your employees. Find out who your internal competition is and neutralize them. They can put you out of business.

THE LESS OBVIOUS

Most CEO's and other business leaders understand the value of internal collaboration. But, a few organizations have subscribed to visibly fostering internal competition. They do it in the belief that it strengthens the organization.

At one time General Electric asked managers to force rank their employees and then fire the bottom 10%. Goldman Sachs periodically selected 500 out of 35,000 employees to be promoted as partners, but many more are weeded out in the process.

Evidence suggests that internal competition generates more morale issues than any productivity gains for the organization. The cost in both human capital and monetary capital is high.

THE MORE OBVIOUS

Even worse than bitter competition among employees, is the not-so-hidden rancor among executives and business partners. Employees will tend to mimic the behavior of their "leaders" and amplify the growing loss of productivity.

When employees compete with each other for their own gains rather than collaborating with each other there are great costs, including:

- Teamwork dies
- Conflicts flare
- Confusion ensues
- Progress slows
- Morale dissipates
- Good people leave
- Weak people stay and poison others
- Creativity caves

Finally, operations slow down, costs go up and profitability bleeds red. Death is near.

THE MOST OBVIOUS

Neutralize and prevent destructive internal competition in order to focus your energy on beating external competition. Here are some practical and proven methods:

Check egos at the door - isolate the negative executives and employees who are the root of internal competition, those who are more interested in personal gain than the greater good of the organization. Give them an opportunity to change, or remove them and replace them with win/win people.

Cultivate win/win - encourage teamwork so that all employees win, rather than just a few isolated "stars."

Hire to values - given the good values of the company, interview and hire employees whose personal values mesh with those of the organization.

Clarify all roles - everyone should have a clearly stated job description with roles and responsibilities. Share them. This eliminates duplication, gaps and uncertainties that can lead to confused competition within.

Build project teams - great satisfaction for all the players comes as the result of watching teamwork work. It defeats internal competition and proves the value of successful collaboration.

Offer incentives - reward teams, both the individuals and the group as a whole. PepsiCo pays 40% of annual bonuses for high performance teamwork.

The evidence of practical experience teaches us that internal competition is costly and dangerous to the sustainable wellbeing of an organization.

THE BOTTOM LINES

Wake up. Internal competitors will destroy businesses faster than external competitors. First, find and dissolve internal competition. Build collaborative teams and reward them for success. Then, focus on dealing effectively with external competition. Beat them.

Lesson: 26

Servant leadership, act two: mentor, teacher, transformer

You would think that servant leadership is one of the latest business trends. Taught in the best business schools, plenty of books, and clips on YouTube. Not so. The concept of servant leadership is referenced in the work of Lao-Tzu, a Chinese philosopher around 500 BC. But, there is more to the story.

It was not until 1970 that an American management consultant and educator, Robert Greenleaf, coined the term, "servant leadership." He gave it definition, promoted it, taught it, wrote about it, and created an awareness of it and its benefits.

INVERTED ORGANIZATION CHART

Overall, servant leadership inverts the typical organizational hierarchy. Leaders are at the bottom and employees at the top. Leaders support the employees. Happy employees create happy customers. Happy customers keep returning and bring new customers with them. The organization succeeds, including employees, leaders, and other stakeholders.

This is the essence of what has been taught and demonstrated about servant leadership for decades – if not longer.

IT REALLY WORKS

One of the best examples of servant leadership in action is the story of Southwest Airlines. 35 continuous years of continuous profitability while other airlines floundered. Their admitted key to success is the passionate support of employees by the leaders. Watch a video clip of Southwest's CEO, Colleen Barrett, being interviewed in the Wharton School of Business at the University of Pennsylvania: https://www.youtube.com/watch?v=6TgR95vnM0c.

THE IMPROVED
SERVANT LEADER

Being nice to employees is essential, but there is far more that some servant leaders are doing for their people: mentoring, teaching, and transforming.

At the beginning of the Southwest takeoff, founder Herb Kelleher discovered a paralegal that worked for Southwest's outside law firm. He eventually hired her into Southwest because he could see the deeper talent in her. Over the course of several years, Kelleher mentored her career, taught her what he knew, and transformed her into his successor. He was beyond just being kind do her and hoping that she would be another happy employee. Today, Colleen Barrett is the CEO of Southwest Airlines.

SERVANT LEADERSHIP UNLEASHED

Creating happy employees alone is a success strategy for any organization. But when servant leaders also mentor, teach, and transform them – magic happens:

Mentoring – a true servant leader takes a personal interest in employees to help them be successful, advance their careers, and feel a greater sense of purpose and contribution to the organization.

Teaching – good servant leaders directly teach employees to help expand their skills, their self worth, and their value to the company.

Transforming – high level servant leaders develop the personal capacities of their employees, including interpersonal communications, life-enhancing knowledge, and the employee's own servant leadership capabilities.

P.S. You do not have to be a hierarchical leader to be a servant leader. All of us can be leaders independent of titles, positions, and whether or not we have people reporting to us. So, if we can be leaders, we might as well be servant leaders.

THE BOTTOM LINES

Serve your employees. Be their servant leader and support their happiness. Watch them better serve customers. See the organization grow and prosper. Don't stop there. Be a better servant leader by mentoring, teaching, and transforming employees. They will better serve you. You will be happy, too.

Lesson: 27

Dodging bullets: risk avoidance and risk mitigation

L eadership gurus offer suggested formulas about how to divide the time spent in running organizations. Dwight Eisenhower, 34th president of the United States, said, "Planning is indispensible." A 2011 article in Inc. Magazine proposed that today strategy is tactics and tactics is strategy. Obviously this division is a sliding scale between winning global wars and software wars. Is there anything else?

Often, a business plan section labeled "Risk Analysis" is parked at the end of the plan, and it is very short. Parked at the end as though it is not important, not necessary, and a "there are no risks" delusional mentality is in front of the organization.

Ask the film camera industry what the risks of Sony digital photography were. Ask any airline what the risks of an airborne bus called Southwest Airlines was. Ask traditional universities what the risk of University of Phoenix online learning became.

UP FRONT

Why not perform an honest risk analysis before starting a new business, or a new product line, or a new service offering? Here are some proven questions to ask that will help get at the root of risks. With the answer to every question, ask another question, "And here is what we can do about it":

- Who else is in this business and what percent of the market do they have?
- What are the three most compelling reasons someone will buy this product?
- Who will buy this service and why?
- What are the three must-have uniqueness's of this business?
- Is there enough market demand to make it worthwhile starting this business?
- What is the breakeven point in terms of units sold and when will that happen?
- How much capital will be needed to launch this business, product, or service?
- Who will be the most likely competitors and why?
- How much production capacity will be needed and when?
- Has valid market research been done?
- What are the follow-on products now in planning that will sustain the business?

AND MORE ...

- How many employees will be needed and when, what are their skill sets, and will they be available in the necessary geographies?

- If this idea were dependent upon one person, what would happen if they leave?
- Are there any potential problems with obtaining enough of the right materials?
- Are there any single-source vendors that could stop production?
- Is there a single part that would prevent the product from being built?
- Are there any potential legal, compliance, or environmental issues?
- What are the geographic considerations, plus and minus?
- Is the business dependent upon a single product or service?
- What if a lively competitor undercuts pricing by 25% or more?
- Who is most likely to be the industry leader?
- What if a competitor acquires another company to take market share?
- What could prevent the business from scaling up and driving costs down?
- Does someone else hold any intellectual property, patents, or trademarks that would be conflicting?

A SHORTENED PATH

If it takes too much time to assess all the above concerns, simply answer this one question: what are the three worst things that could happen and what could be done about each of them? If these questions set off some red lights, beware!

THE BOTTOM LINES

Take a risk (but not the ones that will end the business). Treat risk analysis as a critical part of a business plan. Find out quickly if there are any insurmountable risks. Always imagine the worst that could happen. Prepare for it.

Lesson: 28

The four boxes of leadership: which one are you in?

"**O**ut of the box." Is a business expression for thinking and acting more creatively.

It implies that we are either "in the box" (locked into fixed thinking and behaviors) or "out of the box" (having unconventional thinking and behaviors), and that there is nothing in between or beyond.

Paradox. We are already "in the box" in when we think that there are only two possibilities: in-the-box or out-of the-box.

Not always true.

MORE BOXES

What if there are at least two more variations of the box? That possibility could look like this:

1. *In the box*
2. *Straddle the box*
3. *Out of the box*

4. *No box*

So, what's the application in our real business world?

Here are some general characteristics and examples for these "boxed" ways of thinking and acting.

"In the Box" – Fixed Ways of Getting Things Done

- More rules: solid guidelines about work content and how it must be accomplished
- Little creativity: there is little room for other possibilities
- Focused motivation: people are motivated to do particular work, but not alternatives
- Specific action: time lines are adhered to; fixed quantities of work are expected

Organizations that excel at an in-the-box culture encompass Colgate-Palmolive, IBM, fire departments, highway departments, Swift Trucking and UPS.

"Straddle the Box" – Standard Ways of Doing Things, But with Flexibility

- Some rules: work is done within guidelines, with some situational variations
- More creativity: encouragement to see new possibilities by individuals and groups
- More motivation: permission to express ideas for improved products and services
- Flexible action: some latitude for different actions based upon circumstances

Businesses that are good at standardized approaches to their operations, yet are noted for some elasticity in dealing with customers, include Hyatt, Wendy's, Nordstrom's, Macy's, Citibank and Fidelity.

"Out of the Box" – Unconventional Ways of Thinking and Acting

- Few rules: the environment is largely unrestricted for most work
- High creativity: ideas flow freely and are initially examined for possible use
- Strong motivation: people express ideas and action for continuous improvement
- Rapid action: ideas often move quickly into reality

Companies that have demonstrated out-of-the-box actions include Apple Computer, Amazon, Wal-Mart, Tesla, Costco, FedEx, and Southwest Airlines.

"No Box" - No Precedents, No Rules

- No rules – more spontaneity in an open environment with naturally formed teams
- Maximum creativity – a constant stream of great visions, ideas and possibilities
- High motivation – people work with an unseen energy that is often amazing
- Synchronous action – things happen with stunning speed and accuracy

Entities that exhibited a no-box bent have been Xerox and the discovery of xerography, Intel and the semiconductor, Lockheed's "Skunk Works" and two exotic aircraft with the SR-71 and the U-2, and the U.S. race to the moon.

NO ONE SIZE FITS ALL

Good leaders avoid conforming to one kind of box. They intelligently and intentionally move among all the boxes dynamically as needed and as appropriate. Different divisions, departments and jobs need different ways of operating. The best leaders find the right boxes for each.

THE BOTTOM LINES

Which box? Know what your organization needs. Adapt your leadership style to one or more boxes that optimize effectiveness. You can change as needed. Always know which box works best. And then get in it. Or out of it.

Lesson: 29

The best ways to build trust within your organization

"Trust is the glue of life. It's the most essential ingredient in effective communication."

- STEPHEN COVEY

In successful organizations, leaders, managers, and co-workers trust each other. The players on a sports team trust one another, the coach, and their game plan to succeed. Successful music groups trust their leader and each other.

Trust is the foundation that gives us hope and optimism, and enables us to reach out and take risks.

POWERFUL TRUST-BUILDING EXAMPLES

GOLDCORP
Until 1999, natural resource companies' traditional way of doing business was to keep all maps, statistics and exploration results of their properties very secret.

However, Goldcorp, a gold mining company, ran into a problem that they could not solve:

- They were running out of places to mine gold.
- Tests showed 30 times more unfound gold in their properties.
- They were having trouble finding it.

Goldcorp CEO Rob McEwan made a stunning leadership decision. He asked the head geologist to publicly release all of their geological data as far back as 1948 and display it online - publically. He offered reward to anyone who suggested better ways to locate Goldcorp's reserves.

The contestants identified 110 targets, half of which had not been identified by Goldcorp. Over 80 percent of the new targets yielded substantial quantities of gold. This helped catapult McEwan's underperforming $100 million company into a $9 billion juggernaut.

McEwan demonstrated several essential qualities in building productive relationships: trust, open communications, and flexibility.

NOBU MATSUHISA AND ROBERT DE NIRO

Nobu Matsuhisa opened his first restaurant in Beverley Hills, "Nobu" and it quickly went from obscurity to a star-powered dining experience.

"Nobu" attracted a who's who of Hollywood talent, including one very loyal customer, actor Robert De Niro, who eventually asked Matsuhisa if he would partner with him to open a "Nobu" restaurant in New York City.

But, Matsuhisa was suspicious of taking on a partner and said, "no":

- He had worked for others for his entire life.
- He wanted his own name on a restaurant, unencumbered by anyone.
- By all accounts, "Nobu" was doing well already.

De Niro asked again four years later, having frequented "Nobu" faithfully the entire time. Because De Niro had waited patiently that entire time, Matsuhisa felt very differently. He said, "yes." When asked what had changed his mind, Matsuhisa said:

"I trust him because he was waiting four years." It was De Niro's openness to Matsuhisa's needs and his respect for Nobu's autonomy that allowed this partnership to unfold.

After opening a restaurant in New York, Nobu went on to become a chain of 25 well reviewed, high profile, world renowned restaurants without sacrificing any quality.

SO, HOW CAN WE BUILD TRUST?

Here are three key ideas to amplify trust in an organization:

Know what is important to others – build trusting relationships by showing that you know what matters to others, inside and outside the organization.

Communicate with everyone – have ongoing conversations with others without an agenda in order to build collective possibilities in trusting ways.

Match words and actions – let others see you as trusting and trustful by aligning your communications with the way you behave. Keep your promises.

THE BOTTOM LINES

Take time to trust. Examine your level of trust in others and their level of trust in you. Find opportunities in your organization where more trust would be beneficial. Use honest, trust-building communications and actions in those areas. Trust this.

Lesson: 30

Seven easy steps to more creativity in the workplace

In the world of work and business, creativity is highly valued in most career, job and work settings.

When there is more constructive creativity in well-led organizations, overall business results are typically improved. Innovative products, services and processes are delivered. Teamwork is heightened.

Some questions: How can you improve creativity in your company? Can creativity be learned? Can it be a defined method?

CREATIVE YOU

You are likely more creative than you think you are. Learn how to amplify your natural creativity in your career, job, and work.

Here is a simple creative process that is always available to cultivate creativity. This method can be applied in individual and appropriate group situations. The steps are easy to learn, remember and practice. The time spent with each step is up to you, depending upon the situation and conditions. You can repeat all or some of the steps in given cases. Your intuition will help guide you along the way.

A SEVEN STEP CREATIVE PROCESS

1. Idea
2. Trust
3. Envision
4. Comprehend
5. Discern
6. Appreciate
7. Percolate

Idea – Reserve some quiet, calming time, set an intention to allow spontaneous new notions to emerge and become aware of them. Be open to ideas that might support your business and are often-extraordinary hunches that are not based upon preconceptions. Sometimes these ideas are solutions to problems. At other times they are innovations that can expand a business.

Trust – Gain increasing belief in these ideas with a feeling that they may have a positive effect on your organization. Spend more time with the new notions and consider how they might work in the business.

Envision – Give shape to your ideas by visualizing possible results from implementing them. See this in your mind while beginning to imagine some thoughts, words and actions that could move your mental images into reality. Visualize how your hunches could actually work.

Comprehend – Understand more fully the notions and hunches that are appearing via this process. Ponder these ideas in consideration of new opportunities. Share them with others and get some feedback. Often, inputs from others will enhance the ideas.

Discern – Spend time to clarify how the new ideas might be implemented. Make a conscious effort to avoid over judging fresh ideas while they are still growing and developing. It is equally important to evaluate valid reasons why they might not work.

Appreciate – Experience good feelings about the new possibilities. This adds positive energy to the process for both you and the people around you.

Percolate – Take a break and allow let the new notions to gestate. Later, return to the process and examine if there are additions to any idea. Or, there could be good reasons to terminate an idea based upon timing and practicality.

When it is time to take action, engage your team, form a plan and implement your creative ideas. Utilizing this process can work for products, services, processes, and situations. It is worth your time.

THE BOTTOM LINES

Get creative. Innovative ideas need not always emerge spontaneously. Creativity can be fostered with a seven-step process: idea, trust, envision, comprehend, discern, appreciate, and percolate. Learn the process and start practicing – alone and with teams. Invent great new products, services, and processes. Eureka!

Lesson: 31

Coach, consultant or mentor: which one can help your business?

"So, what is the difference?" you ask.

Coaches facilitate a process in which a business individual is supported while achieving a specific result or goal. Coaches often focus primarily on the personal side of their clients in addition to the business itself.

Consultants typically provide specific skills that the client does not have and does not want to staff with permanent employees. Consultants can install a contemporary IT system, build a strong business plan or providing expert tax advice, as examples.

Mentors engage in a relationship in which their own business expertise and success is used to guide and support leaders to expand their businesses. They build upon the existing strengths of the organization in order to achieve sustainable success.

THE COACH

Qualified coaches typically work with a client from a foundation of goal setting. Then they hold the client accountable by tracking actions and timelines through successful implementation. Often, their coaching is aimed at the client's personal life, rather than business.

To find a good business coach determine that they have enough relevant business experience, understand how they have been trained and know if their coaching is directed at business coaching or personal life coaching.

Good coaches will increase self-confidence and productivity, provide moral support, and teach accountability. They can teach responsibility and offer non-judgmental listening. And, qualified life coaches can help strengthen your personal life.

THE CONSULTANT

The value of good a consultant includes getting expert hands-on advice and actions to resolve specific business issues. They can offer advice, install new business processes, and help upgrade organizational strength. Consultants can recommend ongoing updates. They often work within the organization rather than directly for the CEO.

Critical steps to selecting the right consultant include obtaining referrals, defining the scope of work, getting competitive bids, and establishing milestones for success.

The advantages of contracting with competent consultants include getting experienced skills, avoiding the costs of hiring permanent employees, and acquiring as-needed access to relevant advice. An experienced consultant's perspectives can be very useful.

THE MENTOR

Business mentors are experienced executives with broad based skills in several functional leadership roles. They have strong communication skills including deep listening, plain talk, and ample empathy. Their expert guidance can help clarify vision, mission and values to help build an effective culture.

To find a strong mentor look for successful former senior executives who have excellent references. They are devoted to working with business leaders.

Executives with mentors gain focused support from a "been there, done that" business expert, get a trusted advisor and sounding board, and can absorb the valuable skills and resources of their mentor. Recent research by ATD found that 75% of CEO's said good mentors are critical to their success.

THE BOTTOM LINES

Get some help. Find the greatest obstacle to the long-term growth of your business. Determine if a mentor, consultant or coach best to help you. Find and interview some of them. Engage the one that will help you with your particular situation. Invest in their expertise. Achieve sustainable success.

Lesson: 32

Strategically organize business projects: simply and effectively

> "Great leaders are almost always great simplifiers."
>
> — COLIN POWELL

You have a list of important things to do in your business today and beyond. How do you decide what to do? What is important and what is not? Simply sort your priorities into these four categories: stop, suspend, sustain, and start.

STOP – WHAT PROJECTS TO END

We tend to hang onto familiar activities, products, services and lines of business long after their usefulness. Often, they are money losers, time-drains and consume other valuable resources. In some cases they involve obsolete products and low volume sales

These projects are no longer valuable and likely deserve to be eliminated. Even though they might involve good employees, those people might be good to work on other projects. If not, this can be an opportunity to reduce unnecessary labor costs. Stopping some projects makes more room for new and accelerated ones.

SUSPEND – WHICH ACTIVITIES TO PUT ON HOLD

Some existing projects may have value, but could be consuming too many resources. The timing of introducing new products and services may be too soon or too late. Perhaps there are elements of an activity that are worth preserving for other uses.

Suspended programs could be candidates for spinoffs into other business divisions, or can be sold to an outside company. Some activities that are suspended could optionally be brought back under better conditions.

SUSTAIN – HOW GREAT PROGRAMS CAN BE CONTINUED

If a mainstay part of your business is going well, producing strong revenue, margins and profits, keep it. Not only keep it, examine it to see now it could be tuned up for even greater results. What additional resources does it need to really ramp it up?

Think forward about how these good projects can keep evolving into an ongoing line of products and services. This is a good time for some market surveys to find strengths to build upon and weaknesses to repair. Take very good care of these programs.

START – WHEN IT IS TIME TO START SOMETHING NEW

Most of us get excited about the introduction of new products, services and processes. New initiatives spark the fire of our creative minds. We can inherently believe that these ideas will naturally "take off." But first, what is driving the perceived need for this intended project?

Possibilities include something new bubbling in R&D, a brainstorm in a conference room, marketing demand, competitive pressure, and "no one else is doing it." This is the time for deep discussion and some serious strategizing with a short and simple business plan. If it is a winning idea, assign good resources and get it started.

THE BOTTOM LINES

Organize a list. Consider all the key programs, projects and activities in your organization. Use your teams to build and sort the list into groups using the Stop, Suspend, Sustain, Start guideline. Reach for sustainable success. Act now.

Lesson: 33

Put spiritual ethics and values to work for success in your business

S ometimes called "conscious commerce," companies are increasingly inspired to emphasize higher-order ethics and values in their organizations. This trend is growing. Universities, including Harvard, address it, corporations are opening to it, small businesses see it, and aware people in the workplace express it.

We are moving into an age of work and business where inspired people and organizations focus on values. It is a shift toward more organic and fluent kinds of interactions and spiritually based ethical transactions among people at work.

SPIRITUAL TRANSACTIONS

Beyond and above purely business transactions, a spiritual transaction is a communicated exchange of words and behaviors between people in a work and business setting. These exchanges are built upon spiritually based ethical values, including honesty, trust, respect and compassion.

Spiritual transactions build mutual trust and facilitate good business for everyone. We have the ability to realize that our spiritual nature releases the best in us individually and collectively. We are learning to express our higher inner qualities and accept all the benefits of putting them to work – literally. This has already translated into higher caliber organizations and a business style that is capturing the attention of customers and employees.

ETHICAL ASSETS

Individual and collective values shape our ethical assets. When we use these personal assets in work and business settings the opportunity for individual and group success improves greatly. There is no category on a balance sheet to define ethical assets, yet they are critical to the performance and well being of the business or organization.

Our ethical assets are the foundation of our conscious choices to conduct mutually fair business with our customers, coworkers, vendors, and others in our workplaces – including our online workplaces. These assets are essential to the organization's overall well being.

VALUE ENVIRONMENTS

Do we feel good in certain work and business settings and sometimes wonder why? It might be less about the décor and more about the attitudes and behaviors of the people who work there.

Shared, high value environments develop through the conscious application of our ethical assets and spiritually based transactions.

Value environments are evident in any workplace that is pleasant, uplifting, highly inspired and creative, high value environments embrace strong communications, collaboration, commitment, creativity and compassion. Employees express these qualities for the good of each other, customers, suppliers and the community.

IN PRACTICE
A Harvard Business Review article cites Ricardo Levy, the chairman of Catalytica Energy Systems, about his need for spirituality in business – including decision-making that affects other people. His guidelines are to "quiet the mind, reach deep inside, hear our inner voice, rest with the unknown and stay humble. The right guidance will come."

THE BOTTOM LINES
Build a spiritual base in your business. Develop an environment based on higher values for employees and others. Determine your ethical assets. Decide to foster spiritually-based transactions within your company and with your customers, suppliers and others. It is a good thing.

Lesson: 34

Give the one-minute "elevator speech" for your business a new lift

Have you been frustrated when trying to tell others, within one minute, about your business, and what you are looking for to improve it? Add one simple idea to better engage your audience.

Traditionally, people spend the precious seconds to focus on the good things about their company and then ask for what they need. Few consider offering something of value to their audience at no charge and with no strings attached.

A perennial principle is to give something to others as a way of opening opportunities to receive something from others. Give to get.

So, between first describing your businesses and then immediately asking the audience for something that you want, you can insert a powerful second step - what you can give to the audience on a no-charge basis that could help them.

Your introduction then becomes three easy steps within the 60-second limit: Got, Give, Get.

GOT - WHAT MY BUSINESS IS ABOUT

What is the most important thing you, your business or organization does to help people, clients or industry?

Some examples include: a company that provide a service to diagnose and remove invasive mold from homes and office buildings; a media organization that offers news; another that sells novel snacks and beverage packaging equipment for the hospitality industry.

GIVE - WHAT DO I HAVE TO GIVE AWAY

What will you and your company can freely offer to your audience, remembering that your audience is sometimes just one other person?

From the prior examples: the mold removal company can offer a free inspection; the news organization can give away some printed or digital copies of its publication; the specialized packaging business can hand out samples of its hospitality products.

GET - WHAT RESOURCES I NEED TO HELP MY BUSINESS

What is the one important thing that you and your business need to grow and prosper?

The three example businesses might then ask for: prospects with commercial buildings for the mold removal company; ideas for generating more subscriptions for the publisher; an intellectual property attorney and patent engineer for the unique packaging machinery provider.

The simple added idea of serving others by giving something of value to them as an integral part of your 60-second introduction is effective. It creates more interest in you and your business with both individuals and groups.

THE MAGIC OF GIVING

There is an attracting principle involved. Whenever we are willing to give something of value to others (with no strings attached) it creates some bonding and trust. Subsequent conversations become easier, more interest is created about the giver, and the receiver feels more comfortable.

There is a universal principle involved for the giver as well. Sooner or later the giver will receive something of equal or greater value. It might not come from the recipient of the gift that was given, but it will occur. Especially when the giver is not expecting anything.

This is simply good business. Get it?

THE BOTTOM LINES

Give something away. Write out your 60-second introduction. Use the "Got, Give, Get" cues to describe your business, offer a gift of value and then ask for what you need. Memorize it, start using it and enjoy the benefits. Give and receive.

Lesson: 35

Why "cash is king" from startup to stardom

In the beginning there is cash. It is the real fuel for creating and growing a strong business. Yet, accurate accounting for cash flow was a late show in measuring business health. It is time to tune in about the power of solid cash and where to uncover it.

THE GIANT GREEN CASH MACHINE

A healthy business is a machine that generates positive cash flow, creating more cash than it consumes. Negative cash flow for too long equals bankruptcy.

Income Statements and Balance Sheets long ago became two mainstay tools for recording financial data. The Cash Flow Statement was a late arrival - but a welcome one because it more accurately reports the real availability of cash in the business.

VISIT THE FRIENDLY
CFO OR ACCOUNTANT

A good cash flow statement is something that most of us cannot prepare, but our financial friends can. Business leaders should require it to understand how well their cash machine is running. We might have good-looking income statements and balance sheets, yet not have enough cash to meet payroll. Surprise!

Able accountants will happily help us understand how we are generating cash, where we are consuming it, and what cash we really have – along with suggestions that will help us avoid disasters and improve business.

WILL THE REAL CASH
PLEASE STAND UP?

An income statement can distort liquid cash in several ways, such as the recording of increased sales (orders) that include special deals and discounts. This will raise the cost of sales and lower the net cash revenues (income).

A balance sheet can garble a true cash position when excessive cash is tied up in inventories and accounts receivables. Inventories need to be sold to become accounts receivables, and the receivables must be collected for the actual cash to exist.

An accurate cash flow statement will neutralize the above and other abnormalities.

JACK SAID SO

An icon of strong business leadership, Jack Welch former CEO of General Electric, said, *"Cash is king. Get every drop of cash you can get and hold onto it. That is number one."*

Strong cash reserves help us in many ways, including:

<u>Growth needs.</u> To grow, a company may need to invest in technology, equipment and facilities – and sometimes acquire other companies or pay dividends.

<u>Surviving downturns.</u> A business is better able to survive economic downturns with adequate cash.

<u>Emergencies.</u> Businesses always have unexpected expenses that need to be paid.

<u>Transaction costs.</u> Small businesses need to keep their expenses as low as possible and, by paying with cash, excessive processing fees are eliminated.

<u>Avoiding loans.</u> Many businesses have had to learn the hard way that lenders are becoming more conservative about lending money.

In 2013 the largest U.S. corporate holders of genuine cash net of debt were:

- Apple $16.15 Billion (and the only one with zero debt)
- Chevron $8.03 Billion
- Google $7.57 Billion

- Qualcomm $4.26 Billion
- Amazon $3.70 Billion

A cash-healthy bunch – just ask their shareholders.

THE BOTTOM LINES

Got cash? Ask for accurate cash flow statements from your finance and accounting team. Learn how to read, understand and act upon them. And, in the end there is more cash. Cash is king.

Lesson: 36

See the incredible shrinking business plan in three pages

Is your strategic business plan so thick that it is neither read nor useful? Or does it seem too daunting to even create one? The old three-inch, three-ring binder plans of the past are dead. Learn how to quickly create effective 3-page living business plans.

SPEED COUNTS

The old bulky business plans took an entire staff to prepare them, filled binders, and were for top management only. In fact, they were often labeled, "Secret."

As the pace of business has accelerated, thick plans are often outdated before completed, let alone read and acted upon. Now, with transparent organizations, high-speed communications and shared information, plans are more freely communicated.

But, how do we communicate 100+ page plans? We don't.

MAKE IT SIMPLE
AND SHORT

An effective plan of two to three pages begins with a short outline that covers all the essentials of a workable plan – a plan that can be easily communicated and updated. These sections are written with succinct sentences and brief bullets.

Pages 1 and 2:

Strengths – the three to five most important capabilities, assets, resources and successes your company has to offer its customers and other stakeholders.

Vision – in three sentences, how the company will look in one, two, and three years to the outside world and internally - what benefit the organization will provide to customers and other stakeholders.

Mission – in three sentences, what the business does, why, and for whom.

Values – the top three essential beliefs, attitudes and behaviors by which the organization conducts itself, internally and externally.

Goals – the five to seven highest priority goals that, when achieved, will advance the company to its next level of sustainable success.

Strategy – in one sentence, the overall direction of the business that guides decisions in allocating resources to best achieve the goals.

Actions – five to seven key measurable actions by function (e.g., technology, marketing, sales, customer support, production, others) to achieve the goals – what to do, why, by when, and by whom.

Risks – the top three risks that could negatively impact the implementation of the plan, and how can these risks be avoided and remediated.

Page 3:
Financial - build a short and simple one-page spreadsheet with financial assumptions and projections – such as number of customers, units sold, pricing, income statement, cash flow, balance sheet and capital needs.

SMALL SIZE FITS ALL
This simple plan has been used by small and medium size businesses. Nonprofits, which are non-taxed businesses, can benefit from a flexible three-page plan, too. Some individuals use this format for their one-person businesses as well. If needed, any section of these plans can be separately expanded and detailed as appropriate.

Our business world rolls fast and so should you.

THE BOTTOM LINES
Strategize. Take a day or less with your team to build a three-page strategic business plan that works. Communicate it frequently to your employees and others who can help your business. Review and update it monthly as a living guide for sustainable success. Plan ahead.

Lesson: 37

An open letter to our mentors

What is a mentor? An older, narrow definition is that a mentor is an academic expert who guides us to learn in a university setting. Today's broader definition includes mentors who have helped us in many areas of our careers, jobs and work – and often our lives.

75% of business leaders surveyed by the Association for Talent Development (ATD) in 2012 noted that having good mentors was fundamental to their success.

Take a moment to note some of the mentors who have helped us throughout our professional and personal lives. Let us take time to thank them.

DEAR MENTORS

We could not have succeeded the way we have without you. Our careers, and often our lives, have been enriched by your unselfish devotion to our success. You have been our trusted guides, willing and wise teachers, available sounding boards, and constant cheerleaders.

Thank you beyond measure for all that you do for us, including:

Hiring us into meaningful part-time jobs as kids where we learned something and earned something.

Helping us master our early formal education – kindergarten, grade school and high school.

Guiding us along our college and university paths toward the successful completion of our Associate, Bachelors, Masters and Doctoral degrees.

Being the masterful teacher of what we needed and when we needed it.

Lifting us successfully into our first jobs until we could fly on our own.

Coaching us in establishing a better work/life balance.

Showing us how to create effective win-win relationships with stakeholders in our work environment – customers, vendors, boards and our surrounding community.

Consulting with us about our career and job changes.

Prompting us to have some fun and laughter in our work, and not take ourselves too seriously.

Teaching us beyond the classrooms about the functional areas of our work – business, strategic planning, sales, marketing, service, technology, production, finance and accounting, HR, facilities, and much more.

Answering our many questions, always.

Sharing with us freely your extensive knowledge about business.

Explaining the differences, the similarities, and the relationships between leadership, management and supervision.

Introducing us to valuable people, connections, resources, and creative ideas.

Motivating us to adopt and demonstrate spiritually-based values and principles in all our dealings – ergo, The Golden Rule.

Directing us in effective conflict resolution methods.

Encouraging our lifelong learning by aiming us at appropriate formal and informal venues to learn more.

Convincing us to serve others though acts of kindness, including business-generated philanthropy to our communities.

Serving as our role models when we were experiencing both challenging conditions and successful situations.

Urging us to mentor others by showing us how to share our knowledge and wisdom with others.

Thank you forever,
Your mentees

GIVE BACK
Mentor someone as your "thank you" for what you received from your mentors.

THE BOTTOM LINES
Got mentors? Thank them all in your memories. Send a thank you note or email to the ones who are still around. Give a face-to-face thank you to your current mentors, or the former ones that you periodically see. Be a grateful mentor to others. Pass it on.

Lesson: 38

The five "C's" of creative communications for better business

Both new media and traditional media offer a dazzling collection of how to convey our business communications. We are never without messages to send and receive in all of their many forms. What makes business communications good - or not?

New media such as LinkedIn, Facebook, and Twitter are digital vehicles to convey our business communications - plus digital publications, online advertising, email and texting. Traditional media continues in abundance with print publications, voice messages, postal mail, and even bumper stickers.

What is essential in both new and traditional business messages? Context, Content, Clarity, Color, and Carrier - always.

CONTEXT
Why is the message being sent and what are the surrounding factors, conditions and environment? A straightforward explanation about the purpose of the message is important. Most recipients

won't look further unless they understand why they are receiving the communication in the first place.

CONTENT

What is the message, what does it convey in facts and feelings, and what is the intended call-to-action for the reader? The content must be quickly and efficiently delivered to the intended audience without unnecessary, extraneous added information. Most messages, particularly marketing content, should be informative, engaging, and with a call to action for the recipient - and an easy way for them to respond.

CLARITY

How does the message read or sound, it is uncluttered and understandable, and does it entice the recipient to want more information? Brevity counts, whether the communication is written – visual or audio. Effective messages are simple, easy to comprehend, and not offensive. Experts suggest crafting messages at a mid to late grade school level to improve effectiveness and durability.

COLOR

Who looks at the message and what do they need to see or hear for maximum attraction to the information being conveyed? We know that great art is even better when it has a great frame. Use interesting fonts, graphics, colors, photos, and sounds to enhance the message and engage recipients – but without cluttering and confusing the main message or driving the recipient away. Tasteful design counts, even in audio messages.

CARRIER

Where does the message travel in order to best reach the intended audience? While media cost is a factor, the age, location and other demographics of the recipients help determine choices of new media or traditional media as the carrier. Sometimes, a well concocted mixed media program, such as some social media along with some printed or voice messages can be particularly effective.

No surprise: companies long recognized for durable, effective marketing and another messages include Coca-Cola, Wendy's, Nike, Volkswagen, and Apple.

Need help? Outside communications experts can boost an effective media program by addressing all five C's.

THE BOTTOM LINES

Communicate creatively. Construct marketing and other messages effectively by using the 5 C's as a guide: Context, Content, Clarity, Color and Carrier. Make the messages simple, engaging, easy to comprehend, and with calls to action. Get more business. Clearly.

Lesson: 39

Can't get no satisfaction (in my job)

We've known for years that over 50% of U.S. employees dislike their job. Now, Gallup research tells us that 70% are disengaged from their work. The cost is $550 billion – over one-half of the 2013 total profits of the Fortune 500 companies. Why?

> "'Cause I try and I try... some useless information...
> supposed to fire my imagination... oh no, no, no."
>
> - ROLLING STONES

INFO ABOUT USELESSNESS

Disengaged employees may no longer trust information they receive from leaders. They have dying or dead aspirations. They have lost hope, feel stuck and are not challenged. They do not see progress for themselves and their organization.

Some more reasons for disengagement:

- Entitlement is an outgrowth of our "I deserve more now" culture, but too many employees are unwilling to work for the "more."
- Disenchanted workers may dislike management or others. "People quit people, not companies," signals why some employees emotionally quit, but physically stay.
- Boredom and burnout both play a role. The unchallenged employees rot on the job, and the overworked and under-recognized drift into apathetic "what's the use?"

FIRING THEIR IMAGINATION

Gallup stated that engaged employees "are involved in, enthusiastic about, and committed to their work – and contribute to their organization in a positive manner."

Employee engagement stems from a sense of empowerment and a feeling of connection with the organization – fitting in. When leaders help their people find a place to work, and find their place with work, great progress is made.

Progress is a top reason why employees feel engaged - they are moving forward in their job and helping their organization.

A ROLLING STONE GATHERS NO MOSS

Leaders take action. Here are some effective ways to re-engage employees and to engage new hires:

Replace ineffective managers – hire great managers who are effective at engaging others. Employees will be more productive and satisfied, and business will grow. The cost of maintaining disengaged workers will shrink.

Show promotional paths – most employees want to see a potential path of progress and promotion. They need hope for the future.

Provide more training – this gives employees a boost in their knowledge and skills, and they appreciate being recognized as valuable to the organization.

Get to know employees – remember as many names as possible and find out about their personal lives. This fosters a sense of belonging and helps neutralize the negative effects of a vertical hierarchy.

Find out "why" – not only understand what employees want, but find out why they want it. This gives great perspective about why people want to stay and give their best effort. And, more will be learned about what is causing disengagement.

Build a motivational workplace – treat everyone fairly, allow employees to be creative, foster some humor, make it conducive for employees to give extra effort for the common good of the organization.

More simply put, caring attitudes and actions by leaders engage employees.

THE BOTTOM LINES

Build engagement. Find out what employees need and why. Fire their imagination with motivating actions so they are involved, enthusiastic, and committed to their work. They will contribute to the organization in a positive manner. End disengagement.

Lesson: 40

Three effective ways to keep your business resolutions

A resolution without action is, well, a resolution. And, resolutions can be made at anytime, not just on New Year's Day. They also can be broken at any time and most are. Researchers tell us that less than 10% of resolutions are kept. Worse, only 5% of Americans have goals. What is wrong?

There are key reasons at the outset why our resolutions (aka, intentions or goals) are not kept. In fact, most fail within 30 days due to:

Obscure resolutions – our intentions are vague, non-specific, ill thought out, and can be an avoidance of commitment.

Excessive goals – we become zealots, over committed, trying to show off by having too many resolutions, or having ones that are too difficult, or both.

No action plan – we may have good resolutions in mind, but we have not documented them with specific steps, milestones, and planned completion dates.

If so, we have failed before we start.

MAKING YOUR SELF-PROMISES COME TRUE

When we make resolutions to suit others, we may not do so well. But, when we establish goals to improve our own abilities as leaders, managers, and business individuals, we perform better because we are making a promise to ourselves.

1. CREATING RESOLUTIONS

Examine your roles, responsibilities, and interactions with your organization. Make a short list of the high impact improvements you can make yourself. Find the ones that will improve both you and your business. Make them a stretch, but reasonably doable.

Include both professional resolutions and personal goals. Usually, good personal goals can improve your business - and your personal life, too. Confirm them with a good business mentor or an accountability partner and get their inputs.

Three good resolutions are far better than 10 meaningless or impossible goals. Write your resolutions so that they are specific about what, why and when with measurable milestones. E.g., "I will meet with each of my direct reports for lunch every quarter."

2. IMPLEMENTING RESOLUTIONS

Keep your sheet of resolutions in view and review them weekly. Make appropriate adjustments along the way. Do not become apathetic about them – remember that your resolutions should be a serious promise to yourself.

Weekly, visualize each resolution being worked on and see each being completed successfully. Feel the positive emotions that you will experience as you cross the finish line with each goal. The spoken word has energy, so consider speaking each resolution aloud.

Monitor and measure your progress with each resolution. Make some observations and a few notes about how you see some changes in yourself and any impacts on your organization. Validate your progress with your mentor, coach, or others.

3. COMPLETING RESOLUTIONS

Each time you complete a milestone, celebrate your success. Share your success with others in your organization, your family or your friends. This creates encouragement to continue with all resolutions until they are fully completed. Celebrate again, especially with those who helped you.

Take advantage of your strong momentum. After completing a resolution, create another one – don't wait until next January 1st.

THE BOTTOM LINES

Be resolute. Create, implement, and complete a few meaningful resolutions that will help you and your organization. Be specific, add measurable milestones and track them weekly. Celebrate completing every resolution and then add a new one. Do it now.

Lesson: 41

Merger: the turtle and the rabbit combine companies

We all remember the outcome of the race announced by Aesop the Greek storyteller circa 600 BC. The slow but straight line steady beat of the tortoise won the race against the faster but erratic path of the hare. Remind you of any companies? Here is the rest of the story.

After the race, the rabbit invited the turtle out for a beer. They talked about their respective companies in the competitive forest. They discussed the merits and morals of the race. Then, they reviewed a video of the race.

Eureka! They simultaneously understood that if they combined their strengths and mitigated their weaknesses they could win all the races against other creatures that owned businesses in the same woodland.

THE BOTTOM LINE: #1
Focus and perseverance produces success. Thomas Edison ran thousands of experiments in order to produce a working light bulb

that could be mass-produced. Most others would have run a few experiments and given up. Focus and perseverance is how we graduated with good grades in school – while some of our friends graduated from a local pub. If a second race had been run the rabbit would have recovered from his humiliating first performance, run like he knew how, and won paws down. But, there is more.

THE BOTTOM LINE: #2

Talent, focus and working in your area of expertise produce huge successes. The turtle and the rabbit discussed that, if the turtle had picked the path of other race, a body of water would have been included. The rabbit would have taken off like a shot, but stalled at the edge of the water while the turtle swam across and won again. Steve Jobs consistently used his own and others abilities to swim around competition and singularly innovate successive winning products that users became addicted to. Hold on, there is even more.

THE BOTTOM LINE: #3

Combined talent, focus and a team working in their area of expertise are unstoppable. Having moved from being competitors to being great friends, the amphibian and the bunny spun up a new strategy. They decided to merge their strengths, mitigate their weaknesses and team up for upcoming races. In the next race the rabbit carried the turtle at high speed up to the body of water, the turtle carried his hairy buddy across the pond, and then the rabbit resumed racing to the finish, again carrying his new business partner. Disney was the steady beat business year after year. Pixar was the fast paced innovator of new motion picture media. Together, they have become a tiger in the entertainment jungle.

It would have taken a long time for the rabbit to master swimming, and an even longer time for the turtle to move faster. Instead of overcoming their weaknesses, they amplified their strengths. Gallup Corporation's bestselling book, *Soar with Your Strengths,* illustrates this so well.

In the end, Aesop became a business consultant. Those ancient Greeks were very wise, weren't they?

THE BOTTOM LINES
Get ready, get set, go. In the competitive race with your business are you going it alone with slow progress? Perhaps on of your competitors would consider being merged in as a partner to amplify each other's strengths. This kind of synergy can win big. Really big.

Lesson: 42

Welcome to the new one-person marketing department

O nce relegated as the spare tire of sales, marketing is now the engine in the sales supercar. Marketing evolved from an unknown phenomenon in the early 1900s to a prominent force in the 1950s. By year 2000 marketing power shaped sales. Now digital marketing is the turbocharger.

Marketing is big business for big business, but how can smaller organizations build more marketing muscle?

SKINNY MARKETING
Lesser size organizations can afford at least one experienced person to organize and lead marketing. This inside marketing master can seek and select a great outside team of marketing experts from different disciplines.

The inside marketing guru becomes the integrator and driver of the external resources. The cost of using outside experts is akin to buying what is needed by the slice – and not paying more.

There are no permanent employee costs including hiring and overhead expenses.

EXPERTS ON CALL

There are thousands of experienced marketing experts who operate alone and in small groups. They specialize in specific areas of marketing, and usually have long and relevant experience. Here are only a few marketing elements that can be served by outside experts:

Public relation – providing media contacts to build visibility and credibility for their clients.

Web based marketing – deep knowhow in utilizing the Internet for multiple purposes.

Website development – design, implementation, maintenance, and hosting for effective complex and simple sites.

Social media marketing – expertise in utilizing LinkedIn, Facebook, Twitter, and other newer tools for many aspects of marketing.

Branding – the ability to develop strong statements, engaging language, attractive logos, and other means to evoke positive feelings about their client companies.

Photography/Videography – artistically and technically creating pictorial imagery to enhance marketing messages and engage viewers, both still images and video.

Printing – printed material is alive and well at trade shows, seminars, workshops and other handout-happy venues.

Market and competitive research – with massive files of information, and access to even more, market analysts can provide a wide range of valuable information about intended (and unintended) markets.

Marketing strategy and plans – they figure out an optimum overall direction for clients in view of sales objectives, and then lay out a series of actions that will achieve the goals.

Graphics design – creating attractive logos and other graphics that appear in websites, printed material, ads, public relations, and other media.

SEO (search engine optimization) – organizing and developing content so that search engines bring the client's website and another information to the top of resulting searches by prospective customers.

There are many more facets of marketing provided by qualified outside experts: test marketing, advertising, competitive analysis, content marketing, product marketing, loyalty programs, mobile marketing, events, and more Decide what you need and you will find it.

THE HOME RUN HITTERS

Companies with effective marketing include Apple, Nike, Budweiser, FedEx, Southwest Airlines, IBM and Toyota. Yes, they have big staffs to create the big bang - but they and smaller organizations can achieve proportionately the same results by using outside experts.

THE BOTTOM LINES

Start power marketing. Build a great team of outside marketing performers around a great inside marketing ringmaster. Select experts from different disciplines and buy by-the-slice for only what you need. Keep costs down and gain flexibility. Go to market fast.

Lesson: 43

Pop! Goes the weasel hacker into your customer database

Oh, yes. You have up-to-date antivirus and anti-malware protection in your servers, tablets, laptops, and you have firewalls. Feel safe? Think again. The question is not if an adept, malevolent hacker will breach your system. The question is when. And then what will you do? Pray.

Or, you can install the newest methods of instant response to even a hint of a potential or an actual breach. Call it automated cyber security operations and incident response. And then in real-time, these new systems and your cyber response team can take instant action to thwart and mitigate potentially massive damage to your business and your customers.

The first installations have begun in major corporations and in government organizations.

WHAT WENT WRONG WHEN ...

Target Corporation experienced a well-known breach that did significant damage to a good U.S. company – huge costs, loss of customer data, loss of business, and large collateral damage in the press. Target had conventional breach prevention measures in place, but it happened anyway. Estimated overall costs now exceed several hundred million dollars.

Sony was hit twice with significant breaches that damaged its reputation and loaded it with enormous costs estimated at several hundred million dollars.

For a long list of year 2014 breaches in well known U.S. corporations alone, go to: http://www.heritage.org/research/reports/2014/10/cyber-attacks-on-us-companies-in-2014

This is a list of only the commercial business community. Other lists of breaches in U.S. government organizations are equally mind-breaking.

FROM REACTIVE TO PROACTIVE

Assume that you will eventually be hit with a serious breach, no matter what protective measures you have taken. If you already have your internal cyber security response team in place, good. If not, bad. Go hire a strong team quickly – and give them a great leader.

Then, make very certain that you have the very best anti-virus, anti-malware, firewalls, and other critical components in place.

Either your own cyber response team can do this, or you can contract with outside experts to help.

Finally, start looking for the very best incident response and automated security operations software system. It should integrate at least three critical functions:

Incident Response – informs and marshals your internal security operations teams around a potential or real breach to stop or mitigate economic and other damage.

Vulnerability Management – a process of remediating vulnerabilities based upon your system assets, such as servers, peripherals, laptops, phones, tablets, and more.

Threat Management – provides your system with access to massive databases of known malware samples and viral threats to help isolate the characteristics of a breach.

By the way, this database has been created by the Georgia Institute of Technology and is expanding at the rate of thousands of new entries per day. Do you think we have a problem, Houston?

BREACH COST ESCALATION

The longer a breach persists, the more it grows and the more damage it causes. At some point, your customer databases may be copied without you knowing it. Once that has happened, the economic and collateral damage have skyrocketed and it is literally too late. There is no hope.

So, dig deeper and find out more about the new advanced systems that respond instantly and robustly to potential and real intrusions. Now there is hope.

THE BOTTOM LINES

Get smart. Arm yourself with an expert cyber team to help disarm breaches when they happen. Mobilize them with the newest security operations automation that integrates vulnerability management, incident management, and threat management. Stop digital damage instantly. Trap the weasel hacker.

Lesson: 44

The 3D leader: doing things effectively

Dizzying. The workload crush is on and you are in a mental-emotional free fall. Before you start doing something, there is something else to do, first. It is time to stop and deal with "The Do List." Divide the list and get the right things done right.

What if you do not have to do it all yourself? In fact, what if some of it does not have to be done at all? Here is a fast and effective method to deal with your ever escalating workload.

Drop, Delegate, Do is your new management mantra.

DROP
First, go thought the entire list and rank every action, top to bottom. Put the most important items at the top of the list, and the least important last. No ties allowed.

The truth is that every do list has multiple entries that will go unnoticed if they are never started. Our natural tendency is to declare everything as being important. Or, we think that all actions are of equal importance. They are not. Prioritize.

Now, drop the bottom third of the list. Cross it out. You will never miss it.

DELEGATE

On to more important things. Mark the remaining list as follows: beside every item write either "Delegate" or "Do." You should wind up with about one-half the list in the "Delegate" category and the other half in the "Do" bunch.

For every item that you will be delegating to someone, record the name of that person and tentatively note when you want it to be completed. You might need to first negotiate that completion date, but when it is settled, record it.

Get together with each of your delegate-ees and get their actions started. And, do not forget to track every action through completion. This is called "management."

DO

By now you should have stopped sweating. Only the remaining one-third of the original list is yours to do. Some of these things will be more important than others. So, re-rank them top to bottom. Now, get to work starting at the top.

Sure, new possibilities for action will show up. You can apply the same Drop, Delegate, Do principle to every one of them. Sometimes, you will need to stop something of lesser importance to accommodate a new action of more importance.

Minimize this trading-card effect, though, and follow through on your established list of actions. Management guru Steven Covey taught us to focus on the important, rather than on the urgent.

DELAY: THE FOURTH DIMENSION

Yes, there is a fourth category beyond Drop, Delegate and Do. Go back to your wastebasket and retrieve your tear-stained Drop list. For the few items that you simply cannot part with, re-label them as Delay. Park this Delay list out of sight and out of mind. But, occasionally have a look at it and see if one of these potential actions ensnares you to the point of adding it to your Delegate or Do lists. Oh, and Drop everything you can at any time.

THE BOTTOM LINES

3-D your workload. Learn to purge and re-order your endless "The Do List" in order to get more done – with less fragmentation of your mind. Drop the least important, Delegate the appropriate to your team, and Do your own list. Be known as an efficient and effective 3-D leader. Go do it now.

Lesson: 45

Debrief: what can we learn from our losses?

Oh, oh. Things did not go the way we planned. It was a loss – loss of a sale, key employee, lawsuit, important project, or something else. Do we hide the loss and say, "Oh well, on to the next opportunity (and perhaps another potential loss)"? Or, we can wisely take time to understand our mistakes so that we might improve our future. Hold informative debriefings. Learn and lead.

Most leaders, managers, and individuals prefer to ignore a loss because it seems to be embarrassing, painful, and unnecessary. And, they do not want to waste time to have a debriefing meeting. Blissful ignorance.

Yet, for the wise this is a platinum opportunity to help avoid future losses.

A WORD FROM THE WISE

> "It's often been said that you learn more from
> losing than you do from winning. I think, if

you're wise, you learn from both. You learn a lot from a loss. You learn what is it that we're not doing to get to where we want to go. It really gets your attention and it really motivates the work ethic of your team when you're not doing well."

— Morgan Wooten, basketball coach, lifetime record 1,274 to 192.

CONSTRUCTIVE DEBRIEFINGS

Here are some guidelines to help form good debrief meetings:

Rule 1 – Do it soon. Before everyone forgets the details of a loss, hold a meeting in person, by phone, or by videoconference.

Rule 2 – Invite the right people. Chose those who were involved in the loss, have valuable insights to contribute, and who can learn from the experience.

Rule 3 – No finger pointing. Don't accuse anybody of anything so that everyone feels safe in sharing his or her inputs and ideas.

Rule 4 – Capture the inputs. Share this document with the team and with others in the organization so that everyone, including leaders, can improve.

THAT IS A GOOD QUESTION

These are effective queries to ask in a good debriefing session:

- What was the situation?
- What was our objective?
- How did our team communicate with each other?
- How did lack of trust influence the outcome?
- Where were any mismatches of people, products, or capabilities?
- What could we have done differently?
- Were our expectations unrealistic?
- How could leadership have helped?
- What did we fail to know beforehand?
- How could we have better planned?
- What were the three greatest obstacles we faced?
- How did we respond to each of them?
- Was there competition, internal or external?
- What were our organizational weaknesses?
- What time constraints were challenging?
- Were our goals clear and understandable?
- What other solutions could we have used?
- What are the three most important things we have learned?
- How will we do it differently in the future?
- What did we do well?

And, at the end of the session ask group members if they have any other questions or ideas.

WHY DID WE WIN?

So why not consider a good debriefing for a win? The same questions will apply. There is always more to be learned to amplify the things that went well.

THE BOTTOM LINES

Don't ignore a loss. Assume nothing. Hold a good debriefing meeting and ask great questions without blame. Find out why the loss happened and let the team see how to do better next time. Learn and lead.

Lesson: 46

Ears unplugged: leaders listen with a purpose

Huh? Would you say that again? I wasn't listening. Better leaders, managers, and individuals are better listeners. But, good listeners are in the minority. In business, this can be a big negative. When we do not focus on what others are saying to us, we miss an opportunity to be receptive, to learn, to be deeply involved in the business, to show respect. And, to be respected.

How many times have you been told that you don't seem to be listening? And, have you ever heard a song, but cannot remember any part of some meaningful lyrics? You were hearing the music, but not listening to the words. You "tuned out."

HEARING AND LISTENING DIFFER

You might be hearing a customer, an employee, or the person you work for. But, if you are not actively listening and absorbing their message, too bad – especially if you missed something critical to your job.

We think of communications as writing, reading, and speaking. The missing member of the communications quartet is listening. Even silence is a variation of listening. The statement, "Your silence is deafening," carries an important message.

Yes, we need to hear in order to listen. However, hearing is sensory, listening is mental. Hearing is involuntary, listening is active. Hearing is automatic, listening is purposeful. Get the difference?

REMOVE YOUR EARPLUGS

Here are some reasons why we are ineffective listeners, even without knowing it:

Purpose – we were never taught the value of active listening.
Family culture – everyone tried to talk at once.
Ego – always thinking of the next thing to say while someone is talking.
Time – we are always in a rush and do not take time to actively listen.
Effort – it takes more energy to deeply listen than to talk.
Load – it seems too much to remember what is being said.
Education – we have not been taught how to listen effectively.

Most schools, colleges, and universities do not teach effective, active listening. How many listening courses, formal or informal, have you attended in your life?

Industry recognized the importance of good listening. Xerox developed a series of listening courses for their employees. They copied the course for others.

SHUT UP AND LISTEN

Stop hearing words and start listening to messages. If you have not learned how to listen actively for maximum benefit to you, the speaker, and your organization, here are ten tips:

1. Look at the speaker with eye contact.
2. Let your posture help show interest in what is being communicated.
3. Get rid of every distraction, including mobile devices.
4. Make key mental notes along the way (or use a notepad if you must).
5. Use gestures to show your attention; nod your head or say, "yes."
6. Add some prompts, such as "Then what happened?"
7. Do not think about what you are going to say next.
8. Focus only on what the speaker is saying; let stray thoughts go.
9. Be patient, open-minded and avoid assumptions.
10. Let the speaker completely finish before you respond in any way.

You can do it. We listen much faster than we talk. Research proves it.

THE BOTTOM LINES

Listen up. Stop talking and start listening. Learn how to listen effectively. You will get the message, really. Learn more and interact positively with others. It is good business. Better leaders listen better. Shhhhh.

Lesson: 47

Leadership, karma, and the reason for everything

Good happens. Bad happens. In the life of a business, we are happier when perceived good is happening, and we are down when the bad is winning. What is causing the good or the bad? Philosophy, history, and contemporary evidence suggest that we are, not the external world. Leaders, managers, and individuals who understand this can intentionally create good businesses. Try it.

Try treating customers, employees, and others poorly on a sustained basis and watch what happens. The business, the organization, growth and profits decline sooner or later. Bad happens. In the end, you lose.

Treat everyone with good products and services, fair pricing, and kindness, and the enterprise will more likely succeed. Good happens. You win.

KARMA BALANCE

Put aside past lives, reincarnation, and religious precepts. Remember that the universe is strung together with something other than string and adhesive tape. Yet, everything is in balance and has been for billions of years.

Karma is the idea that however we have acted to date plays out in our current world. True in business. Being a good leader, manager, or individual contributing to a strong business in the past accumulates "good karma," which creates more benefits now and into the future. Lead a business poorly, accumulate "bad karma," and things will get worse, sooner or later. Negative balance.

Business news, articles, and columns portray philanthropic people – some of little or average means, and some with billions of dollars. They spread good to help others just for the sake of helping them. This creates good karma, and equal or greater good will be returned to them, somehow, someday. Positive balance.

Call this a universal spiritual principle.

THE GOLDEN RULE

Don't like karma? Here is another universal spiritual principle that accomplishes the same thing: *"Do unto others whatever you would have them do unto you."*

This message exists in virtually every culture in the world. Treat others well, and we will be treated well going forward. And the corollary is that, if we are unkind to others, we will be treated accordingly in the time ahead.

In business, the Golden Rule, like karma, works just as well. Be conscious of your persisting thoughts, words, and actions toward your employees, customers, and others. Choose the positive every time.

TARGET EXAMPLE

Target Corporation's founder believed that, "Success is making ourselves useful in the world, valuable to society, helping in lifting the level of humanity." He began giving 5% of Target's profits to community causes.

By the end of 2012, Target was giving $4 million every week to the communities it serves – to resolve hunger, help disaster preparedness and relief, support the arts, and put more youth on the road to high school completion. Target is committed to giving $1 billion for education by the end of 2015.

Community giving is a win-win situation for Target: "When we help build strong communities, our customers and employees who live there help us build a strong business."

SIMPLER YET

Karma and Golden Rule too complicated? Try "Like attracts like."

THE BOTTOM LINES

Collect good karma. Follow the Golden Rule. Treat employees, customers, and others the way you want to be treated. Give generously of your funds, care, and products. What you give will come back multiplied. Your business wins. Everybody wins. You win, too.

Lesson: 47

Why nonprofits are really for-profit businesses

Wait. Before you stop giving to your favorite nonprofits, don't you want them to be healthy financially? Do not give to make them healthy – give to keep them healthy. The best nonprofits are run like good businesses. You are making an investment in organizations that support good causes. You would not invest in a bad business. Would you?

Astute donors (particularly philanthropists) want to know about the business side of the nonprofits that they support. This can include strategic business plans, financial reports, and major programs.

The overall effectiveness of nonprofits to those they serve is a compelling reason to donate to the organization. Or not.

WHO'S IN CHARGE?

Most nonprofits have many or all the elements of a for-profit business:

Leadership – a competent, experienced, compensated expert. The same leadership qualities of a business apply to a nonprofit.

Organization – how the nonprofit functions, communicates, and dedicates itself. This is essential to efficiency, productivity, and quality service to those it serves.

Marketing – advertising, public relations, social media, websites, search engine optimization, emails, and more. These build its constituency and donor base.

"Sales" – often called Development in nonprofits. It is key to contact with existing and potential donors in order to fund the organization and its work.

Production – some nonprofits have in-house printing facilities and other production needs. This can be faster and less expensive than outsourcing.

Facilities – many nonprofits own extensive buildings, campuses, and land. These are assets that can grow in value to help the organization.

Human Resources – virtually all HR policies apply to nonprofits, including recruiting, training, benefit programs, and community relations.

DOLLARS AND SENSE

Yes, nonprofits have the same finance and accounting departments as for-profit businesses. They, too, deal with payroll, accounts payable, accounts receivable, purchasing, and investments. They file standard financial reports with state and federal agencies, just like for profit businesses.

A well run nonprofit will generate a financial surplus (profit), but is obligated to utilize the surplus to strengthen the organization and provide added support for its constituency. There are no shareholders and no distribution of surplus to them. Consequently, the nonprofit pays no taxes.

Effectiveness is measured in many ways, including the percentage of donor dollars spent on programs that support their constituency vs. the percentage spent to run the organization.

COMPETITION?
Surprise! Most nonprofits face competition. This includes universities, churches, and welfare organizations. It may be another organization in a similar role. More often, it is simply competing at-large for donor dollars in general.

THE GOOD AND THE UGLY
Unity is a respected nonprofit in Kansas City, which supports the spiritual well being of over 2,000,000 people. It has all the attributes of a good business. Its lifeblood is a strong and durable donor base. The effectiveness of Unity has sustained its durability and growth – for over 125 years.

Breast Cancer Society of Mesa, Arizona is a newer nonprofit that has gone bad. Recently, its leaders scammed $187 million from donations for personal use, and gave little to actual cancer patients. Federal action has closed it down. Ugly.

THE BOTTOM LINES

Give generously. But give to durable, healthy nonprofits that are well organized with strong leadership. Help sustain these organizations based upon their continuing effectiveness. Know that their financial surplus is necessary. Do good.

Lesson: 49

Build it, buy it, or bury it?

Yᵒᵘ have a problem. You need an important resource, but cannot decide how to secure it. Time, trouble, and talent are key factors. So are costs, confidence, and capacity. Your required resource can involve a product, a part, a process, or a person. A knee-jerk reaction is usually to do the easiest thing, or the fastest, or the least cost. So, what to do?

Options include sit on it and do nothing, ask a friend, search the Internet for a solution, or wait until next quarter. Typically, these will not solve the issue. What will?

Hint: look at three possibilities. Build it yourself, buy it from someone else, or bury the idea because it was not a good one in the first place.

BUILD IT
Well, yes, you cannot "build" a needed human resource, but you can hire one. You can build a product or part. And, you can build a new process or refine one.

Before you decide to build the resource yourself, answer these questions:

1. How important is this, really?
2. What will I have to give up?
3. Who will be in charge of this?
4. What other assets will be involved?
5. How much time will this take?
6. Who will create the plan for this and when will the plan be complete?
7. What is the total cost?
8. What are the top three risks?
9. Would it be better to purchase this?
10. What value will this add to the organization?

Now, ask your team to evaluate the findings. Then put it aside momentarily.

BUY IT

You have fully assessed the possibility of building your needed resource. Now it is time to examine the cost-benefit of procuring the resource from outside the organization.

Again, a series of questions will help evaluate the situation and contribute to better decision-making:

- What are the possible sources?
- When would the resource be available?
- How much will it cost?
- What will happen if the supplier is late?

- What are the major risks and consequences if it does not work?
- Is this a permanent, temporary, or intermittent need?
- Do you have a known supplier that you trust?
- Who will create the specifications for what you need?
- Do you have a staff member who will drive this procurement?
- What else have you not thought about?

Ask your team to evaluate these findings. Compare the information about building the resource inside to the analysis of buying the resource from the outside. Which looks better? Before implementing your decision to build or buy, there is another possibility. Hang on.

BURY IT
Was there anything in your information about either building or buying the resource that suggests that the entire idea is a weak one? If so, there are some options to consider:

Cancel the project?
Delay the project?
Change the project?
Put it on the shelf for now?
Consider a hybrid build/buy – build part of it and buy some of it?

Or, finally kill it and put it to rest forever. Amen.

THE BOTTOM LINES
Make a decision. An educated one. First, consider building a needed resource yourself. Next, take a look at purchasing the resource. Compare the two. Then, is it worth doing it at all? If not, bury it. Now decide.

Lesson: 50

Qualify, qualify, qualify: the secret to sales success

S low win, no win. Why does it take so long to get an order? Why does someone else get the order? Why does no one get the order? Why does a buyer tell us we have the order, and then the deal evaporates? These are questions that too many sales people have – particularly when their expected commissions are low. Or zero.

Sales productivity is a function of how many leads, the quality of the leads, turning more leads into true prospects, and increasing the odds of getting orders.

No time to waste. Successful selling is a process of productivity. Well-intended sales people want to maximize their time and get orders as efficiently as possible. How?

ORGANIZING THE ODDS

In a sense, a sale is a game of odds, so keep the odds in your favor. This can be done effectively through a series of simple, constructive questions to your intended buyers – and to yourself. First, let's clarify a few terms.

A *lead* is a person or organization that might be a candidate to purchase products and services from you and your company. The odds at this point are near zero.

A *prospect* is a lead that has been qualified as one that is worth pursuing for business. Ooops – make that pre-qualified.

YOU MEAN DO IT AGAIN?

So, you thought (or were taught) that prospect qualification is a one-time event. Ergo, ask a few questions in the first contact with a sales lead, and then the potential customer is qualified as a prospect. Think again.

Things change: the prospect's needs change, your primary contact is reorganized or moves, the prospect's financial situation shifts, there is new management, the prospect's business is acquired. Your prospect is a moving target.

Therefore, keep qualifying throughout the sales cycle. In fact, keep qualifying until the prospects pay you for their purchase. Afterward, qualify them for more business. Never stop qualifying. Ever.

QUALIFICATION IS
THE QUESTION

Here are some powerful, popular, and proven qualification questions to ask during your sales cycle – important, more important, hugely important, and most important:

IMPORTANT

Is this a lead or a prospect, and why?

What are they using today that you might replace?

What is their level of maturity, knowledge, and capability?

Who are the competitors; their strengths their weaknesses?

What are your product's three greatest strengths and weaknesses?

MORE IMPORTANT

What are they most concerned about; what are they looking for?

What is their pain, what is their fear?

Do you really have something to sell that will satisfy their requirements?

Does your product/service pricing fit within the buyer's budget?

Are there any issues with how they would adopt or install your product/service?

HUGELY IMPORTANT

Who are the recommenders?

Who is the decision maker?

Who is the order signer?

Do they have the budgeted funds?

Will they buy in a reasonable time frame?

MOST IMPORTANT

All things considered, will this prospect really purchase from you?

Any time that too many of the answers are not in your favor, consider bailing out of the situation. Instead, spend your time wisely and find better prospects.

THE BOTTOM LINES

Qualify. Do not waste time selling into an impossible situation, especially to prove how good you are. Sell to real prospects where you can succeed. Constant qualification is critical. Ask a lot of questions, often. Keep qualifying. Win.

Lesson: 51

Lost leaders of the rut:
organizational rot

How shocking. You wake up one day and find that your business is dying. Headed for the grave. In a rut. It happened without notice – and without you noticing it. As you survey the situation a question forms, and then an answer. What happened? Stagnation.

Something changed and it was not you. It was the market, or technology, or competition, or costs. Perhaps you lost your creative innovation. Maybe you were so successful that you became complacent. Or, all the above.

> **The only difference between a rut and a grave**
> **are the dimensions.**
>
> – ELLEN GLASGOW, AMERICAN AUTHOR.

SYMPTOMS AND REMEDIES

In diagnosing the disease of "organizational rot," there are some warning signs – much like the human body. These signals can foretell a fall into the abyss of failure – yet there are proven remedies:

Command – the leader of a growing business has stopped leading. There is a weakening of the essential things that created a good business: vision, mission, values, strategy and execution. It is time to regenerate the business.

Apathy – loss of passion, complacency and its deadly companion, "there is no competition," are killers. Leaders must re-awaken the organization and themselves, instilling an energetic fresh sense of newness and excitement

People – a once vibrant company can suffer from bad hiring practices and keeping poor performing employees too long. Reassess the organization and replace weak spots with great new people. Train and upgrade the team.

Atrophy – products and services have aged, not staying ahead of market needs. Ensure constant teamwork among marketing, development and production. Get great new products to market, fast.

Instability – no defined standards and no controls. Critical information is received too late. Communicate expectations and track actual performance against standards. Report results and celebrate goal achievements.

Blindness – marketing fails to understand and address a rapidly shifting market and customer base. Good products became positioned poorly against competition. Update marketing and sales programs.

Service – customers receive little respect and weak service. Their needs are not understood and met. Demand that the sales and service teams care deeply for customers. It costs less to keep a customer than to find a new one.

Money – there is not enough cash via loans, investors, cash flow, and other means to sustain or accelerate growth. Implement a plan with resources to generate cash and investments. Build up cash before you need it.

Technology – IT systems may be outdated, too complex and not best serve the organization. Manual procedures and training are misaligned with the IT system. Good IT is essential and must be continuously assessed and upgraded.

Inflexibility – dogmatic adherence to what has worked to date, and failure to believe that constant change is mandatory. Always assess the entire business environment, internally and externally, and make appropriate changes.

Including the leader.

FOLLOW THE LEADER

Your team likely has followed you into the ditch while you were dozing. But, your alarm clock has gone off. Organize the team;

decide what to do and how to do it. Then start. But, hang on to your vision – it is a permanent ladder to success.

THE BOTTOM LINES

Wake up. Get out of stagnation. Stop digging and start doing. Move quickly with your team. Find and diagnose the issues, strategize, lay out an action plan both near term and longer range. Climb out of the ditch together. You first.

Lesson: 52

How to avoid death by meaningless meetings

Zzzzzzz. You dozed off in another meeting. Got tired of an un-structured talkathon. Worse, there were too many slides with too much information and obscure graphs. And, the presenter read the information on the slides. No audience interaction. No Q&A time. Burned an hour and left with nothing. Zero.

And, there is a real financial cost. Example: if an organization holds four one-hour meaningless meetings per day with 10 average-compensation attendees, the annual cost is about $250,000 – a quarter-million. In larger companies these kinds of meetings are a multi-million dollar loss.

Then, double the loss? Yes, because these employees are not working on something else that has value.

THE NEW MEETING PLAYBOOK

The more obvious things to do for meetings with meat are easy and effective:

- Announce the meeting well in advance so that the right people will be there.
- Pre-publish the agenda – no agenda, no meeting.
- Include the date, time, place, and the objectives of the meeting, location and length of the meeting, and a list of the attendees. Plus any materials the attendees must bring to the meeting.
- Minimize the length of the meeting – if 20 or 30 minutes will work, why bother to schedule the "automatic hour" that is so common.
- Stay on topic – stick to the agenda and push other items to later meetings.
- Stop unnecessary, non-productive, sidebar conversations.
- Leave time for group discussion and Q&A – and end on time, every time.

Follow every meeting with brief meeting notes and any action items. Publish these (and do not forget to thank the attendees).

NEXT SLIDE PLEASE

To support good meetings, demand great presentations. And today that means superb slide decks, which include:

Brevity counts – spend no more time presenting than three minutes per slide. This says that there should be no more than 20 slides in a one-hour presentation.

Simplicity rules – keep slide backgrounds and text simple and uncluttered – they are easier to read and are not distracting. Make sure that they can be read from the back of the room.

Limit text – put no more than five lines ("bullets") on each slide (plus the slide headings). And, have only three to five words per line. Slides are meant to be major talking points for the presentation.

Clarify graphs – make them simple, clean, and easy to see. Have only one or two charts per slide. Explain the charts as part of the presentation.

Minimize "cute stuff" – use sound and motion sparingly. They can burn time and cause loss of interest.

Read not – point to items on the slides, but do not read the slides. Treat the slide text as items to be discussed and to help guide the flow of the presentation.

Give handouts – copies of slides are perfect notepads for the audience to record their notes.

The best slide decks generate interest, help guide the flow of the presentation, and are a list of important things to discuss.

Remember that good slides should support great presentations – not be the presentation.

THE BOTTOM LINES

Stimulate audiences. Prepare for and hold meaningful meetings with valuable outcomes. Create agendas that draw attendees. Manage meetings. Add simple slide decks that support strong presentations. Publish meeting notes and action items. Save money. Get results.

How to Order More Books

The author, Tom Zender, hopes that you enjoyed this book.

Additional copies of *The Bottom Lines 2016: 52 Unforgettable Lessons in Leadership* by author Tom Zender can be ordered at Amazon.com. Both the paper and digital e-book versions are available.

Tom Zender
tomzender@me.com
www.tomzendermentor.com